ESL TEACHER'S HOLIDAY ACTIVITIES KIT

ESL TEACHER'S HOLIDAY ACTIVITIES KIT

Elizabeth Claire

Illustrated by: Daniel Shelton
Phil Singer
David Swanson
Kevin Tinsley
Brad Vancata

**THE CENTER FOR APPLIED
RESEARCH IN EDUCATION**
West Nyack, New York 10995

10 9 8 7 6 5 4

Library of Congress Cataloging-in-Publication Data

Claire, Elizabeth.
    ESL teacher's holiday activities kit / Elizabeth Claire;
illustrated by Daniel Shelton . . . [et al.].
        p.   cm.
    ISBN 0-87628-305-9
    1. English language—Study and teaching—Foreign speakers.
2. Holidays—United States—Exercises, recitations, etc.   I. Title.
PE1128.A2C518   1990
428′.007—dc20   90-41346
                                                          CIP

ISBN 0-87628-305-9

**THE CENTER FOR APPLIED
RESEARCH IN EDUCATION**
BUSINESS & PROFESSIONAL DIVISION
A division of Simon & Schuster
West Nyack, New York 10995

Printed in the United States of America

Dedication

To Aunt Aggie, who brought love, fun, and homemade *kiffles*
to our family holidays

—and to volunteers of the Holiday Project

You are the gift.

Acknowledgements

A book of this scope owes a great deal to many people. I would like to particularly thank Dick Buehler for his ESL expertise in reading the preliminary manuscript. Bea Pfeffer, Christina Theodoropolos, Terri Lehmann, Susan Simms, Nadine Simms, Marc Rosen, and Sandy Intorre contributed ideas and confirmations of ethnic holiday celebrations, for which I am grateful. Thanks to Maria Maier, Hazel Buckwald, Mayra Mateos, and Honey Wada for feedback on field testing some of the lessons. Many fond thanks to Mark Lieberman for encouragement, discipline, bagels, editing, and details too numerous to mention.

Thanks to Debby Kurtz for the painstaking care needed to coordinate the many parts and pieces of this kit and for launching the production; to Jan Douglas for her competent, caring and knowledgeable copyediting, and Zsuzsa Neff for managing the many details of design and production as well as holding my hand during the final months of pre-publication tasks.

My gratitude also to Werner Erhard, for the energy and inspiration provided by his partnership in the Education Network (the antidote to "teacher burnout"). Thank you also, Werner, for inventing the Holiday Project and giving all of us the opportunity to participate in it.

About the Author

Elizabeth Claire graduated magna cum laude from the City College of New York and won an Experienced Teacher's Fellowship to New York University, where she got her M.A. in TESOL. She taught English as a Second Language for twenty years to students of all ages and backgrounds, including ten years in Fort Lee, New Jersey, elementary schools and seven years in New York City secondary schools. She has authored ten other books, including *ESL Teacher's Activity Kit* (Prentice-Hall), *The ESL Wonder Workbooks, A Foreign Student's Guide to Dangerous English, Three Little Words:* A, An, *and* The, *and* *What's So Funny? A Foreign Student's Introduction to American Humor.* She lives in Saddle Brook, New Jersey and is currently a freelance materials writer and ESL consultant and is the president of Eardley Publications.

About This Kit

The *ESL Teacher's Holiday Activities Kit* is a unique resource for busy teachers of students with limited English-speaking ability. In it you will find complete, ready-to-use lessons and activities to introduce over forty holidays and special events celebrated in the United States. The more than 175 reproducible pages allow you to tailor-make lessons for building important language skills and teaching holiday concepts. These lessons are ideal for beginning and intermediate students in elementary, secondary, or adult education classes.

Activity pages are provided for each holiday. For those holidays which traditionally receive a lot of attention in American schools (Halloween, Thanksgiving, and Christmas, for example), and important ethnic holidays (Passover, Black History Month), you will find eight to fourteen activity pages from which to choose. Minor holidays and other calendar events such as United Nations Day, Inauguration Day, Susan B. Anthony Day, Fire Prevention Week, and the seasons are also included, each with one to four activity pages.

The *ESL Teacher's Holiday Activities Kit* includes:

- Background information for teachers on the holidays
- Over 500 illustrations depicting essential holiday vocabulary, including thirty full-page illustrations which can be used as coloring activities for younger students
- Reading selections on holiday stories, holiday customs, and the origins of each holiday, including:
  — vocabulary builders
  — close exercises
  — multiple choice comprehension checks
  — reading reinforcement activities
  — discussion starters
  — listening skills exercises
  — practice with key grammatical structures
  — quizzes and tests

- Strategies for incorporating "natural way" (whole student/whole language) techniques in teaching about holidays, with complete sample lesson plans
- Activities for "natural way" language acquisition including:
  — total physical response activities
  — holiday games
  — arts and crafts projects
  — gifts to make for the holidays
  — taking part in holiday celebrations
- Holiday songs, puzzles, mazes, and word games
- Opportunities for students to share their native holidays, customs, and activities with classmates in order to build self-esteem and international understanding

Special features make the lessons and activities in this resource easy for you and your students to use.

- Hundreds of illustrations help clarify new concepts.
- Each major holiday has lessons for beginning and intermediate students.
- Sentence structures are controlled.
- High frequency vocabulary is used. Key words and idioms that may be new to students are repeated several times in the text. They appear in a separate word list, as well as in vocabulary exercises.
- All items are numbered to help students keep their place in the lessons.
- The *Kit* is organized according to the school year, starting with September.
- Each lesson is self-contained. You may select and skip lessons based on your students' needs.
- Answers to puzzles are provided at the end of this kit.

The *ESL Teacher's Holiday Activities Kit* presents a general picture of holidays in the United States. We hope these pages will serve as a springboard for helping your students enjoy the regional, ethnic, and family variations of holidays as they are celebrated in your locality.

Elizabeth Claire

How to Use This Kit

The following tips will help you meet your students' needs most effectively.

1. Decide how much instructional time you want to spend on a particular holiday and its activities. Before the holiday occurs plan your teaching schedule to allow for this time. Decorate your room or have a bulletin board display of the coming holiday.

    Younger students can create a monthly calendar showing the dates of the upcoming special days. Older students can receive an oral preview of each month. This will alert students to the preparations others are making for the holiday and allow for maximum motivation and a natural reinforcement of the language and information learned.

2. Select the pages that will meet the needs of your students and duplicate them. You may want to enlarge some pages if your copymachine has this capacity. The *ESL Teacher's Holiday Activities Kit* provides materials that allow for a "spiral approach" to learning about the holidays. In the second year of a program, students can learn additional information and concepts relating to each holiday topic.

    NOTE: You may want to shorten a lesson or omit information for a variety of reasons. To do this, cover the areas of the student pages that you do not want to use with a strip of paper before duplicating. You can easily remove the paper to duplicate the entire page for future use. You can also type or write in additional information before duplicating, such as labels for the illustrations.

3. For lessons of several pages, you can create booklets using the full-page illustrations provided in the kit as covers. These full-page illustrations can be used a motivating discussion starters and vocabulary builders. They may also be used as coloring activities for younger students. Ask students to help collate and staple the booklets. Three-ring binders may also be used to hold the pages together. To do this, duplicate the pages onto three-hole punched paper or punch holes after the booklets have been collated.

4. For beginners, present material orally using "comprehensible input" first, that is, use actions, real objects, and illustrations to convey meaning. Use English and nonverbal clues to convey meaning as much as you can to promote thinking in English. Where meaning is abstract or ambiguous and

cannot be understood through pictures, actions, or context, students should be encouraged to use their bilingual dictionaries.

OPTIONAL: Make a copy of the page that includes the word list for the reading lesson you are teaching. Write the native-language definitions next to each word in the list, or ask a bilingual assistant to do it. Then duplicate the page. You can do this for each native language represented in your class.

5. Color the illustrations in the book and create decorations and pictures for the classroom.

6. You might want to create an answer key on copies of the exercise pages to use when correcting student work. This will make it easy to delegate the correction of routing assignments to students.

7. For intermediate students, extended information on some holidays is provided with background information that ties into history lessons. You may want to spend more time on reading, writing, vocabulary building, and structural patterns with your intermediate students. One way to do this is to initiate discussions of holidays celebrated in your students' native countries that are similar to U.S. holidays. The readings can be prepared for homework assignments, and students themselves can be responsible for new vocabulary.

8. Check your school library or media center for movies, filmstrips or video programs about the holidays. You can compensate for language and reading limitations of your students by using a lot of visuals.

9. Role-play events and activities related to the holidays.

10. Invite native-English-speaking students from other classes to come into your class to tell how a holiday is celebrated in their families and to answer questions.

11. Celebrate holidays in your classroom. Bring in or have the class prepare traditional foods; play holiday games; dress in traditional holiday clothing. Play "Holiday Bingo." Plan additional ways for students to take part in holiday celebrations at school or in the community.

12. Collect magazine pictures and take your own photographs of holiday celebrations. Build a photo file for future years. If you have access to a video camera, make videotapes of holiday celebrations.

13. Check television guides and notify students of any programs that will add to their enjoyment or understanding of holidays. Assign programs to watch for homework or, if VCRs are available, tape the programs and watch them in class or during lunch time.

14. Encourage students to express their reactions to the U.S. holidays.

15. Have students introduce their own holidays of the season or variations in customs. Duplicate appropriate pages for student use.

Contents

TECHNIQUES FOR TEACHING LISTENING AND SPEAKING

It is easy to make a language lesson difficult. Language learners can easily become overloaded and then "tune out" as soon as they are faced with a sentence they don't understand. What takes skill on the part of the teacher is to make the lessons easy and meaningful without being dull. Students who feel smart learn faster!

Listening, when meanings are made clear, is the most rapid road to language acquisition. Students benefit from an overall sense of the sounds, rhythms, and structure of the language as well as from attention to small, bite-sized chunks. The more a student hears and *distinguishes* what he or she hears, the faster the approach to fluency and grammatical accuracy. If you elicit simple feedback from students as you present new material, it will help them to distinguish the meanings and essential elements in the new sound patterns they are hearing. Feedback may be as simple as a nod, an action, or a one-word answer. New material should be presented in easily manageable chunks to ensure low anxiety and high motivation. Keep in mind that each student progresses at his or her own pace, and "manageable chunk" can mean something different for each student.

A beginner's language acquisition will be slowed down if s/he is asked to frequently produce or repeat sentences before they are heard a sufficient number of times. *Hearing the teacher repeat a new sentence several times is more effective in ultimate student production than having students repeat sentences themselves the same number of times!* Speaking puts a student on display; she or he is publicly tested for tongue-muscle coordination, memory of the sounds and the order of sounds to be produced, timing, rhythm, and intonation. In addition, the student is grappling with interference from native language sounds, structures, and rhythms. The first thing that is sacrificed is the connection of sound to meaning.

Errors in speaking will arise because of native-language interference, difficulties with our sound system, inadequate vocabulary, and striving to communicate on a level that is too complex for the learner. In "natural way" teaching, error correction does not interrupt the flow of communication. Instead, you acknowledge the content of the student's message and include the correct or missing words in your response. At some point, you might want to drill the students on useful structures, but not when you are in the middle of a conversation or lesson focusing on *content*. Support speaking, don't squelch it. For example, if a student says, "Me no like pumpkin pie," you might say, "Really? I don't like pumpkin pie either" or "I like pumpkin pie, but I don't like cranberry sauce." Make a note to schedule a few five-minute drills on "I like/I don't like" constructions using vocabulary from the content you are discussing. If the student continues to make this error in free conversation after drilling, you can stop, raise an eyebrow, and let the student self-correct.

In a stimulating and encouraging environment filled with opportunities for listening to comprehensible language, you can create the confidence and the situations that generate the desire to speak. Build your students' confidence and provide them with the right situations, and they will reward you with more rapid learning.

TEACHING READING, WRITING, AND VOCABULARY

You will need to employ a variety of techniques to meet the needs of students of different ages, levels of native language literacy, oral English proficiency, familiarity with the Roman alphabet, and learning styles. Some of your students may be literate in their own language, while others are not. It is possible to teach literacy in a second language when there is none in the first language, but nonliterate students will need to spend a longer amount of time building a listening/comprehending background, and will need individualized help in recognizing letters and their sounds.

Writing is not a separate skill from reading, but a correlate of reading. Good readers make good writers. Conversely, writing helps focus reading skills. *Handwriting,* on the other hand, *is* a separate skill that will need more or less attention depending on the age and previous experience with writing.

The reading selections in the ESL TEACHER'S HOLIDAY ACTIVITIES KIT may contain many words that are new to your students. The amount of material that your class can cover in a lesson will depend greatly on the ratio of new words to known words. You can pre-teach some key words to prepare students for the reading selections. One way to do this is to teach the words *orally* first. Make a list of the new words on the chalkboard and gather pictures or props to describe the words. Point to each picture or prop and act out each word. Then read the words on the chalkboard and have students repeat after you. Other new words can be learned or clarified in the context of the reading selection. Still others may only become clear through a translation or by using a bilingual dictionary.

Here are a "teacher's dozen" ESL reading, writing, and vocabulary-building techniques. You can deepen and reinforce the same material by selecting different techniques when reviewing on following days.

1. Read the material aloud, providing a model of the rhythm and intonation of each sentence. Point to illustrations as they are mentioned. Dramatize any actions. Ask students to listen and, if able, read along silently. (The paragraphs are numbered to help students stay with you as you read.)

2. Ask questions related to the selection that can be answered merely with "yes" or "no." Ask "either/or" questions. Ask questions with one-word answers. Repeat each question until several students have had an opportunity to answer.

3. Read words or sentences from the lesson at random. Have students listen and identify the number of the picture or paragraph to which your words refer.

4. Read and have students repeat chorally or individually after you. Instruct in pronunciation and intonation as needed.

3

5. Read a sentence and then ask students to find the sentence in the reading selection and read the sentence that follows it. This gives practice in skimming.

6. Read the words in the word lists with students repeating after you. Have students find the words in the reading selection and underline them.

7. Ask students to copy the word list in their notebooks and write definitions of the words or use them in sentences.

8. Ask students to read silently, using their bilingual dictionaries to look up unfamiliar words.

9. Call on students to read aloud individually.

10. Ask one student to read aloud while other students role-play the actions.

11. You or a student can role-play an action, while other students locate and read the sentences that describe the action.

12. Match words to sounds, pictures, or synonyms on the blackboard or worksheet.

13. Play Holiday Bingo to reinforce vocabulary, reading, and spelling.

14. Ask students to copy the reading selection, or a portion of it, and then copy key words several times.

15. Create "true/false" sentences based on the material for students to respond to orally, and later in writing.

16. Dictate words or sentences for listening and spelling practice.

17. Have students read to find answers to specific questions and then write down the answers.

18. Create a list of words for a spelling test. Use the words in a sentence from the lesson or a variation on it as you dictate for the test.

BUILDING VOCABULARY RECOGNITION WITH HOLIDAY BINGO

1. Prepare a master blank bingo card on an 8½-by-11-inch sheet of paper. Duplicate enough for each student.

2. Elicit twenty-four words associated with a given holiday from students and write these on the board. Or, take words from the word lists provided in the book. Demonstrate how to write the words at random in the squares so each student will have a card with a different arrangement of words.

3. Cut markers from construction paper or oaktag. Distribute markers to the students. You will need about twenty markers for each student.

4. Write the words on large flash cards. Shuffle the pile of cards and place them face down on the table, or put the cards in a bag and shake it to mix them up. Pick and read the words one at a time.

5. Ask students to use the markers to cover the words you call. When a student has five words in a row covered, he or she says "Bingo!" The student then reads the words in the bingo row as you and the class check them against the words that have been called.

6. Offer small prizes such as raisins, nuts, fruit, candy, erasers, pencils, stickers, warm fuzzies, privileges such as being first in line, and so on. Play each round until there are three or four winners. Play a final round until everyone has had bingo and won a prize.

TEACHING GRAMMAR

Structures are kept simple in the HOLIDAY ACTIVITIES KIT, but they are not presented in a developmental sequence. Sentences are short, but natural verb tenses are used throughout, providing a whole-language approach to learning.

Space does not permit a full range of grammatical lessons to accompany each reading lesson. Most of the reading lessons will lend themselves to exercises on singulars and plurals, present tense singular and plural forms, past forms, *Wh* question forms, negatives, comparatives, superlatives, pronouns, and prepositions. The exercises for beginning students will not require an active familiarity with grammar. Intermediate students answering discussion questions will need assistance with structures.

You can explain and "prescribe" grammar (the traditional approach), or you can use patterns from known material for students to *discover* points of grammar. Using the latter approach, you can create pattern drills for those features of the language that present problems of interference as needed by your students. In this kit the major focus is on content, but we want students to increase grammatical proficiency and fluency as well.

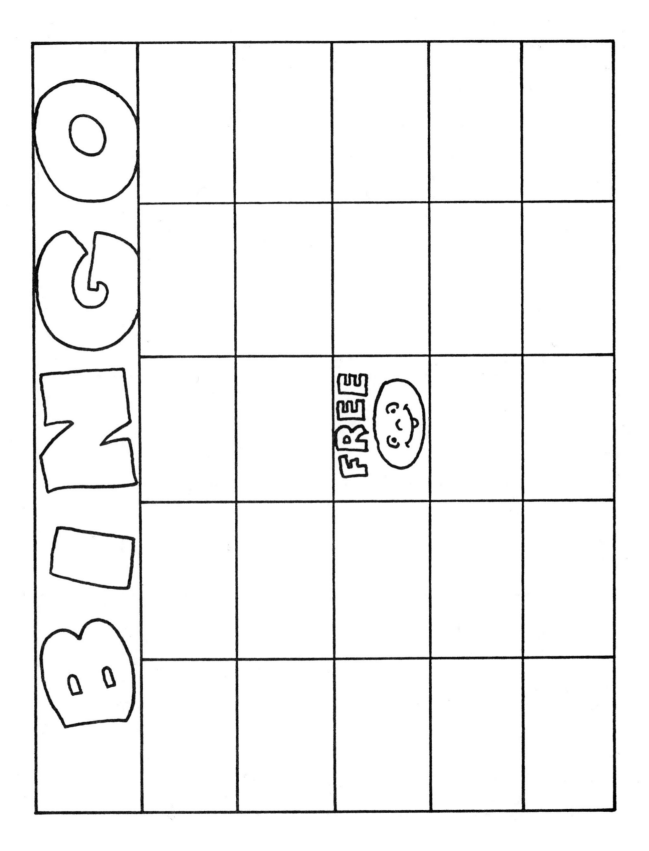

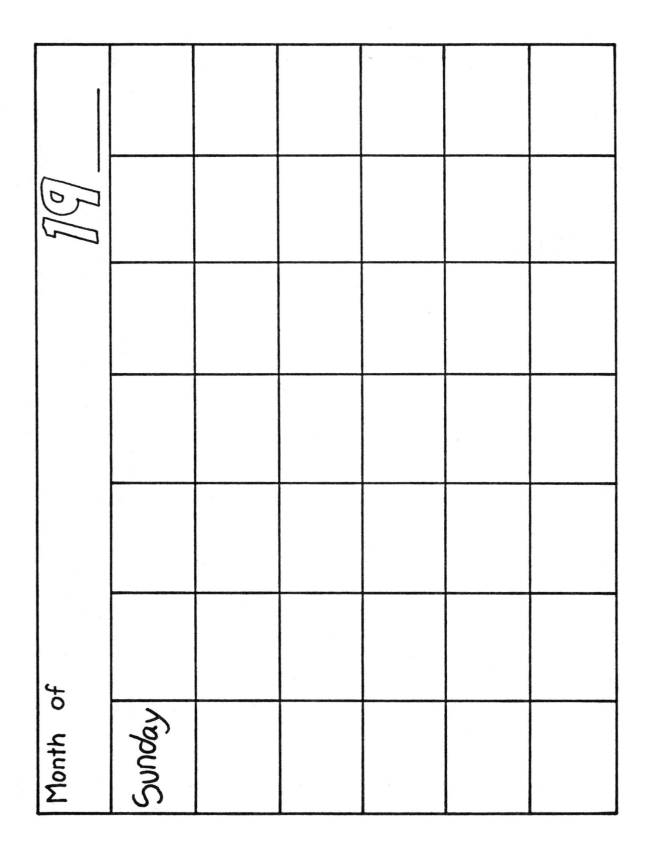

Month of

19___

Sunday

Labor Day is the first Monday in September. On Labor Day we think about the workers of this country.

Can you name these workers in the picture?

1. police officer
2. teacher
3. carpenter
4. truck driver
5. doctor
6. nurse
7. pilot
8. bus driver

ALL ABOUT LABOR DAY

1. Labor Day is the first Monday of September. On this day, we think about the workers of this country.

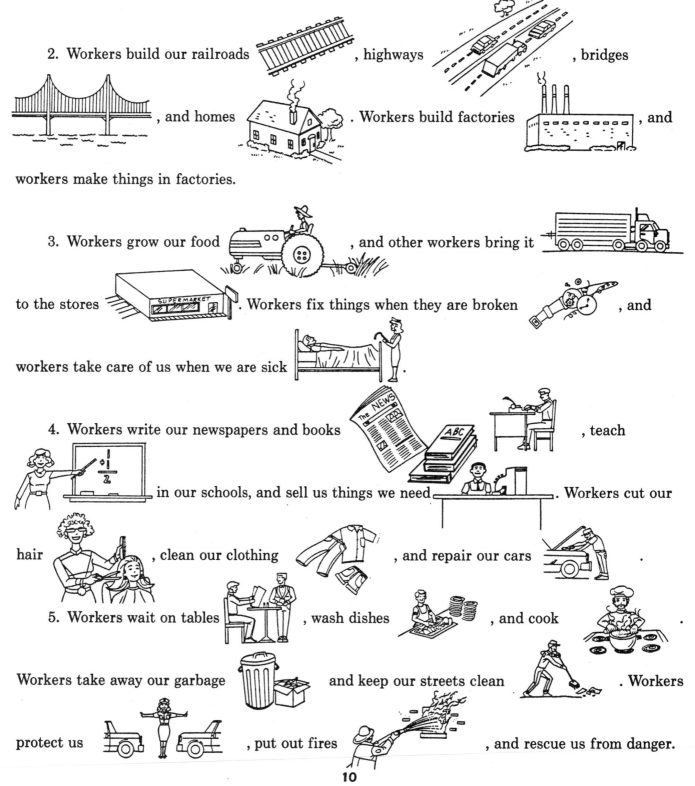

2. Workers build our railroads , highways , bridges , and homes . Workers build factories , and workers make things in factories.

3. Workers grow our food , and other workers bring it to the stores . Workers fix things when they are broken , and workers take care of us when we are sick .

4. Workers write our newspapers and books , teach in our schools, and sell us things we need . Workers cut our hair , clean our clothing , and repair our cars .

5. Workers wait on tables , wash dishes , and cook . Workers take away our garbage and keep our streets clean . Workers protect us , put out fires , and rescue us from danger.

ALL ABOUT LABOR DAY (continued)

6. Today machines 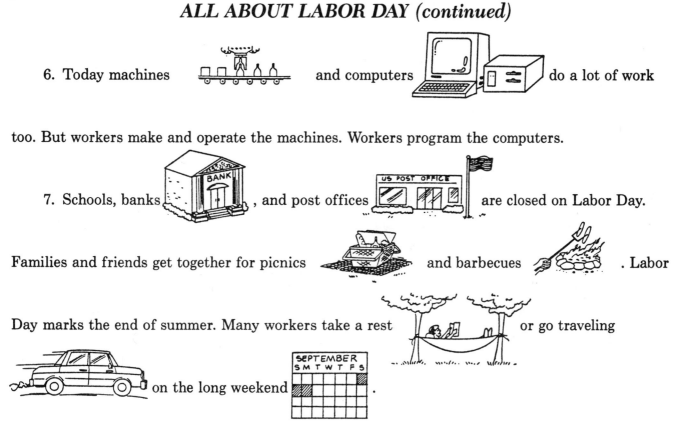 and computers do a lot of work

too. But workers make and operate the machines. Workers program the computers.

7. Schools, banks , and post offices are closed on Labor Day.

Families and friends get together for picnics and barbecues . Labor

Day marks the end of summer. Many workers take a rest or go traveling

on the long weekend .

ALL ABOUT LABOR DAY: EXERCISES

I. Do you know these words? Find the words in the story. Draw a line under them. Copy the words. Write the meanings.

labor	bring/brought	cook
think/thought	store	take/took
worker	garbage	streets
country	fix	protect
build/built	break/broke/broken	put out
railroad	take care of/took care of	rescue
highway	newspaper	danger
bridge	sell/sold	machine
home	clothing	computer
factory/factories	repair	operate
grow food/grew food	wait on tables	program a computer

II. Complete the sentences:

1. Labor Day is the first _____ in September.

2. It is a day to think about _____.

3. Workers do many things for us. They _____

    _____

    _____

4. Machines and _____ do a lot of work, too.

5. We still need _____ to build and operate the machines and to _____ the computers.

6. Schools, banks and post offices are _____ Labor Day.

7. Many people _____ or

    _____ on Labor Day.

III. Can you tell what work these workers do? You can find the answers in the story, "All About Labor Day."

construction workers	barbers	carpenters
sanitation workers	firefighters	farmers
factory workers	mechanics	beauticians
truck drivers	nurses	cleaners
engineers	writers	waiters
computer programmers	teachers	dishwashers
police officers	salespeople	chefs

ALL ABOUT LABOR DAY: EXERCISES (continued)

IV. Answer the questions.

1. What work do you do?

_____

2. What workers are in your family?

_____

3. What workers work in your school?

_____

4. What workers do you meet in your community?

_____

5. What new jobs are there for workers?

_____

6. What kinds of work are not needed today because machines do the work?

_____

WORKER MATCH-UP

Match the worker with the job:

1. A plumber _____   A. makes bread, rolls and cake

2. A teacher _____   B. flies a plane

3. A baker ____   C. builds houses

4. A mechanic _____   D. helps students learn

5. A secretary _____   E. programs computers

6. An executive _____   F. manages an office

7. A driver _____   G. drives a truck, bus, or taxi

8. A pilot _____   H. fixes water pipes

9. A carpenter _____   I. waits on tables

10. A computer programmer _____   J. works in an office

11. A waiter or waitress _____   K. fixes cars and machines

12. A _____ _____.

© 1990 by Elizabeth Claire

THE HISTORY OF WORKERS IN THE UNITED STATES

1. One hundred years ago, life was very hard for most workers. Many people worked twelve or fourteen hours a day. They worked six days a week. Their wages were very low.

2. Working conditions were not safe. People got hurt or killed in accidents at work. Young children worked in factories and in coal mines.

3. Workers lost their jobs if they complained. Then their families went hungry.

4. Workers joined with other workers. They formed unions. The unions asked for safe working conditions. They asked for shorter hours. They asked for higher pay.

5. Many owners of factories and mines were rich and powerful. They said unions were against the law. They put union leaders in jail. They fired workers who joined a union. They killed some union leaders.

6. Some unions went on strike. The workers said, "We won't work until we have better conditions."

7. The owners hired workers who were not in the unions. They hired armies to fight against the unions.

8. Some strikes lasted a long time. Workers in other unions helped. They collected money for the striking workers.

9. Today there are safety laws for work places. There is a minimum wage law. There are laws that children cannot work in mines or factories. Children must be in school.

10. There is unemployment insurance for workers who lose their jobs. There is social security for workers over age 65. There are pensions for workers who are disabled.

11. Labor Day celebrates all workers. It reminds us that workers are important.

THE HISTORY OF WORKERS IN THE UNITED STATES: EXERCISES

I. Do you know these words? Find the words in the story. Draw a line under them. Copy the words. Write the meanings.

wages	job	safety
working conditions	hungry	law
safe	join	work place
hurt	union	minimum
kill	short/shorter	unemployment
accident	owner	insurance
young	power/powerful	social security
factory	go/went on strike	pension
coal mine	until	celebrate
afraid	hire	remind
lose/lost	collect	

II. Answer the questions below:

1. How many days a week do workers work in your native country? _____

2. How many hours a day? _____

3. Is there a minimum wage? _____

4. Are unions legal in your native country? _____

5. Are there laws about children working? _____

6. Is there unemployment insurance for workers who lose their jobs?

    _____

7. Are there good working conditions at your job, or at your parents' jobs?

    _____

8. Is there a special day that celebrates workers in your native country?

    _____

III. Play "Workers' Bingo."

ROSH HASHANA

Rosh Hashana is the Jewish New Year. Jews go to the synagogue on Rosh Hashana. Some schools are closed. Banks and post offices are not closed on Rosh Hashana.

ROSH HASHANA: THE JEWISH NEW YEAR

1. Rosh Hashana is the Jewish New Year. This year Rosh Hashana is on _____.

2. The new day begins when the sun goes down. The new year begins when summer is over.

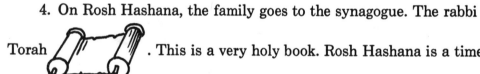

3. Before the new year begins, Jews clean their houses. They buy new clothes. They send cards to friends.

4. On Rosh Hashana, the family goes to the synagogue. The rabbi reads from the Torah . This is a very holy book. Rosh Hashana is a time to think and pray.

5. Jewish families prepare a big dinner for Rosh Hashana. They eat special foods. They eat challah, a special kind of bread. They eat honey cake and fruit. They eat sweet things for a sweet year.

6. For ten days after Rosh Hashana, Jews pray. They ask God to forgive them for any bad things that they have done.

ROSH HASHANA: EXERCISES

I. Do you know these words? Find the words in the story. Draw a line under them. Copy the words. Write the meanings.

Rosh Hashana	synagogue	challah
New Year	rabbi	honey cake
Jewish	the Torah	sweet
begin/began	holy	God
sun	think/thought	forgive/forgave
summer	pray	
over	prepare	

II. Choose the best answer:

1. The Jewish New Year is _____.
   (Rosh Hashana, Labor Day)

2. Jews go to the synagogue to _____.
   (work, pray)

3. A rabbi is a Jewish _____.
   (bread, teacher)

4. The rabbi reads from the _____, a very holy book.
   (Torah, challah)

5. On Rosh Hashana, Jews eat _____.

cards	sweet foods
bad foods	the sun
clothes	fruit
challah	a holy book
	honey cake

III. Answer the questions below:

1. When does the Jewish New Year begin? _____

2. When does a new day begin? _____

3. How do Jews get ready for Rosh Hashana? _____

   _____

4. What do they do on Rosh Hashana? _____

   _____

5. What special foods are eaten on Rosh Hashana? _____

   _____

YOM KIPPUR

1. Yom Kippur comes ten days after Rosh Hashana.

2. It is the holiest and most serious day of the year for Jewish people.

3. Jews rest from work. They go to the synagogue. They pray all day on Yom Kippur. They say prayers for dead people. They light candles.

4. They do not eat or drink anything.

5. At the end of the day, they feel very happy. The new year can begin with a clean heart. When they see the first star, they may eat.

YOM KIPPUR: EXERCISES

I. Do you know these words? Find the words in the story. Draw a line under them. Copy the words. Write the meanings.

Yom Kippur	synagogue	light
after	pray	candle
holy	prayers	heart
serious	dead	star
rest		

II. Choose the best answer:

1. Yom Kippur comes _____ days after Rosh Hashana.
   (ten, twenty)

2. Yom Kippur is a _____ holiday.
   (Christian, Jewish)

3. On Yom Kippur, Jews _____ all day.
   (pray, work)

4. On this day, Jews do not _____ anything.
   (say or do, eat or drink)

5. When they see the first _____, they may eat.
   (star, house)

III. Answer the questions below:

1. What do Jewish people do on Yom Kippur? _____

   _____

2. Do Jews eat any special foods on Yom Kippur? _____

   _____

3. *Think:* Are you sorry for some things you did this year? Can you correct them? Can you plan

   a way to be better next year? _____

   _____

   _____

   _____

   _____

   _____

CITIZENSHIP DAY

1. September 17 is Citizenship Day. The United States Constitution was signed on this day in 1787.

2. Schools, banks and post offices are not closed.

3. People who are born in the United States are citizens. People from other countries can become citizens too. Citizens have rights. Citizens have responsibilities.

4. To become an American citizen, a person must

   a. be 18 years old.

   b. enter the United States legally and live in the country for five years (three years if the person is married to an American citizen).

   c. have a good moral character.

   d. understand basic English.

   e. understand the basic history of the United States.

   f. promise to give up citizenship in the old country.

   g. promise to support the Constitution and obey the laws of the United States.

5. The United States is a democracy. Citizens 18 years or older may vote. Citizens may run for public office. Citizens serve on juries.

CITIZENSHIP DAY: EXERCISES

I. Do you know these words? Find the words in the story. Draw a line under them. Copy the words. Write the meanings.

citizenship	responsibility/-ies	promise
Constitution	enter	give up/gave up
sign	legal	support
school	married	obey
bank	moral	law
post office	character	democracy
be born; was/were born	understand	vote
other countries	basic	run for public office
become/became	English	serve on a jury
rights	history	

II. Answer the questions below:

1 How can someone become a U.S. citizen? ————————————————————

——

2. Do you think it is necessary to understand basic English to be a citizen? ———————— Why

or why not? ——————————————————————————————————

——

3. Why is it necessary to give up citizenship in the old country?

——

4. What are some of the rights of citizens? ———————————————————————

——

5. What are some of the responsibilities of citizens? ——————————————————

——

THE CONSTITUTION

1. England had thirteen colonies in North America.

2. They were Massachusetts, New Hampshire, Connecticut, Rhode Island, New York, New Jersey, Pennsylvania, Delaware, Maryland, Virginia, North Carolina, South Carolina, and Georgia.

3. After the War of Independence (1775–1783), the colonies became free. Now they were thirteen independent states.

4. At first, each state made its own laws. Each state printed its own money. Each state had its own army.

5. The people said, "We need a better system. The states must be united. We must have a constitution."

6. So they decided to have a big meeting in Philadelphia. It was called the Constitutional Convention. The people in the thirteen states sent fifty-five delegates to the Convention.

7. George Washington was the president of the Convention. There were other great men at the Convention too. Benjamin Franklin, Alexander Hamilton, and James Madison were there.

8. It was not easy to write a constitution. The delegates worked for many months. They argued over many things.

9. The delegates from the small states were afraid that the big states would have too much power.

Name _____ Date _____

THE CONSTITUTION (continued)

10. The southern states had slaves. They wanted to keep their slaves. The northern states did not have slaves. They wanted to stop the slave trade.

11. Some delegates wanted to elect the president for life. Others wanted to elect the president for four years, or five years.

12. The delegates studied the laws and the constitutions of other countries. They wanted the best form of government for this country.

13. At last, on September 17, 1787, the Constitution was complete. The thirteen states approved it. It became the law for the United States. George Washington was elected the first president.

14. The delegates did a good job. The Constitution is the basis of our democratic government. It is now over 200 years old. It is the oldest federal constitution in the world.

THE CONSTITUTION: EXERCISES

I. Do you know these words? Find the words in the story. Draw a line under them. Copy the words. Write the meanings.

England	system	slaves
colony	united	north/northern
war	constitution	slave trade
independence	meeting	elect
independent	convention	approve
state	delegate	basis
law	president	democratic
print	argue	form
money	power	government
army	south/southern	federal
		world

II. Answer the questions below:

1. How many colonies did England have in America? _____

2. After the War of Independence, were the states united? _____

3. Why did the people want a constitution? _____

_____

4. Where was the constitutional convention? _____

5. Who was the president of the convention? _____

6. How many men were there? _____

7. What famous men were there? _____

_____

8. Was it easy to write the Constitution? _____

9. What did the delegates argue about? _____

_____

_____

10. When was the Constitution completed? _____

11. Who was elected the first president of the United States?

_____

12. Did the delegates do a good job? _____

THE SEASONS

There are four seasons in the year: spring, summer, fall and winter.

SPRING - MAR 21 - JUN 20

SUMMER   JUNE 21 - SEPT 20

FALL SEPT. 21 - DEC. 20

WINTER DEC. 21 - MAR. 20

FALL

1. On the first day of fall, night and day are equal. The first day of fall is September _____.

2. The weather becomes cooler in the fall.

3. In some parts of the country, leaves turn yellow, red, and brown. They fall off the trees.

4. Grass and many plants die.

5. Wild animals get ready for winter. Some animals eat a lot and get fat. They will sleep all winter.

6. Other animals hide nuts and seeds. Some birds fly south where it will be warm.

Name _____   Date _____

FALL: EXERCISES

I. Do you know these words? Find the words in the story. Draw a line under them. Copy the words. Write the meanings.

fall	country	get ready
first	leaf/leaves	get fat
day	turn red	sleep
night	fall off	winter
equal	tree	hide
weather	grass	nut
become	plant	bird
cool/cooler	die	fly
part	wild	south
	animal	warm

II. Match the words with the correct picture.

1. leaf ___C___   2. grass _____   3. animals _____   4. bird _____

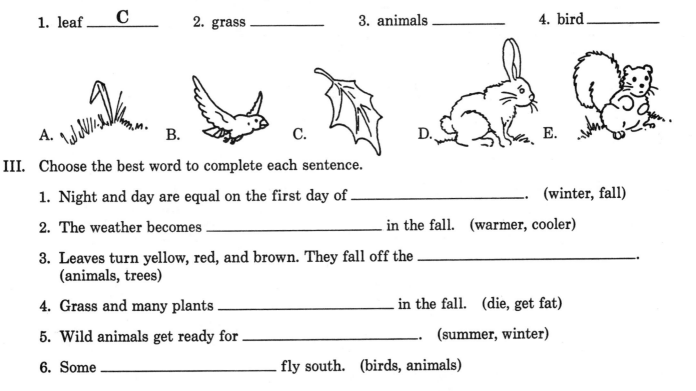

A.   B.   C.   D.   E.

III. Choose the best word to complete each sentence.

1. Night and day are equal on the first day of _____. (winter, fall)

2. The weather becomes _____ in the fall. (warmer, cooler)

3. Leaves turn yellow, red, and brown. They fall off the _____. (animals, trees)

4. Grass and many plants _____ in the fall. (die, get fat)

5. Wild animals get ready for _____. (summer, winter)

6. Some _____ fly south. (birds, animals)

FIRE PREVENTION WEEK

What dangerous conditions can you see in this home?

ALL ABOUT FIRE PREVENTION WEEK

This week is Fire Prevention Week. We can learn to prevent fires. Here are some fire safety rules:

1. Keep matches away from small children.

2. Don't play with fire.

3. Turn off the stove before you leave the house.

4. Don't put too many wires in the same outlet.

5. Don't smoke in bed.

6. Put out matches and cigarettes completely. Do not throw hot matches or cigarettes into a wastebasket.

7. Don't leave wires uncovered.

8. Don't leave paint rags or other oily rags around.

9. Keep a fire extinguisher near the kitchen, but away from the stove.

10. Have a smoke alarm near the bedrooms.

11. Make plans for action in case of fire. Have a fire drill in your house.

12. Plan all possible exits if the main exit is on fire.

13. Plan a place where the family will meet if they leave the house during a fire.

14. Know how to call the fire department.

15. If there is a fire, leave the house immediately. Do not stop to take property.

16. Call the fire department from a safe telephone. Do not go back into the house.

17. If your clothes catch fire, do not run. Roll in the grass.

Name _____ Date _____

FIRE PREVENTION WEEK: EXERCISES AND ACTIVITIES

I. Do you know these words? Find these words in the story. Draw a line under them. Copy the words. Write the meanings.

fire	wires	plan
prevent	outlet	action
prevention	completely	in case of
safe	wastebasket	fire drill
safety	uncovered	exit
rules	paint rags	fire department
matches	oil rag	immediately
stove	extinguisher	catch on fire
turn off	smoke alarm	

II. Match:

1. match _____

2. fire _____

3. stove _____

4. wire _____

5. outlet _____

6. smoke _____

7. fire extinguisher _____

8. smoke alarm _____

9. exit _____

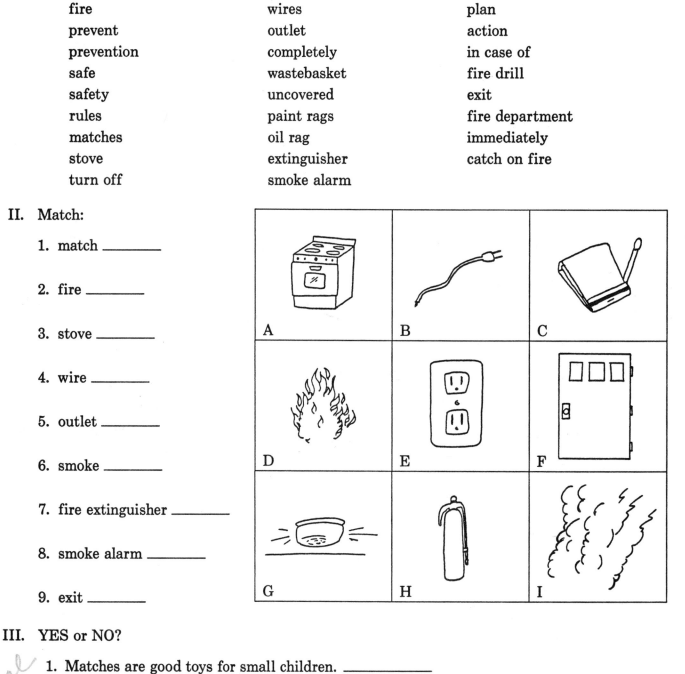

III. YES or NO?

oral

1. Matches are good toys for small children. _____

2. Leave the stove on when you go out to shop. _____

3. Put out matches and cigarettes completely. _____

FIRE PREVENTION WEEK: EXERCISES AND ACTIVITIES *(continued)*

    4. Fires need oxygen and fuel. _____

    5. It's OK to put many wires into the same outlet. _____

    6. Keep a fire extinguisher near the stove. _____

    7. Have a smoke alarm in the kitchen. _____

    8. Plan your exit in case of fire. _____

    9. Know how to call the fire department. _____

  10. If there is a fire, get all your important things before you leave the house. _____

  11. If there is a fire, call the fire department first, then leave the house. _____

  12. If your clothes catch on fire, run as fast as you can. _____

IV. Discussion:

    1. Have you ever seen a fire?

    2. What caused it?

    3. Can you think of other rules to prevent fires?

    4. Can you think of other rules to escape from fires?

COLUMBUS DAY

Columbus discovered America in 1492.

THE STORY OF COLUMBUS DAY

© 1990 by Elizabeth Claire

1. This is America.

2. Native Americans lived here.

3. This is Europe. And this is Asia. Asia is east of Europe.

4. People in Europe wanted to buy things from Asia, or the Indies. They wanted spices, perfume, silk cloth, and gold.

5. It was very difficult to go east to the Indies by land.

6. Christopher Columbus said, "We can go by sea. The world is round. We can sail west and get to the East."

7. Many people said, "It is impossible. You are crazy."

8. Queen Isabella of Spain thought Columbus was right.

9. Queen Isabella gave Columbus three ships and ninety sailors.

10. Columbus sailed west in three little ships: the Niña, the Piñta and the Santa Maria.

11. They sailed for many days. The sailors were afraid. They wanted to go back to Spain.

12. Columbus said "We will find the Indies very soon!"

13. The ships landed in America. The day was October 12, 1492. Columbus thought he was in the Indies. He called the people Indians.

14. Columbus took some Native Americans back to Spain. He took many things. He did not know that he had discovered a new continent.

COLUMBUS DAY: EXERCISES

I. Do you know these words? Find the words in the story. Draw a line under them. Copy the words. Write the meanings.

America	perfume	impossible
Native American	silk	crazy
Europe	cloth	Spain
Asia	gold	ship
East	sea	sailor
Indies	world	afraid
want	round	take/took
buy/bought	sail	discover
spices	west	continent

II. Complete the sentences:

1. People in Europe wanted to buy ——————, ——————, —————— and ——————.

2. It was very difficult to go to the East by ——————.

3. Christopher Columbus said, "We can go by ——————. The world is ——————."

4. "We can sail —————— and get to the East."

5. Many people thought Columbus was ——————.

6. Queen Isabella gave Columbus —————— ships and —————— sailors.

7. Columbus sailed west in three little ships: the ——————, the ——————, and the ——————.

8. The sailors were afraid. They wanted to go back to ——————.

9. Columbus thought he was in ——————. He called the people ——————.

10. Columbus did not know that he had discovered a new ——————.

III. MATCH:

1. Isabella ——————   A. Columbus's ships

2. Christopher Columbus ——————   B. Queen of Spain

3. the Niña, the Piñta, and the Santa Maria ——————   C. discovered America

4. Japan, India, and China ——————   D. Native Americans

5. Indians ——————   E. countries in Asia

6. perfume ——————   F. make food taste good

7. spices ——————   G. can be made into clothing

8. silk cloth ——————   H. smells good

COLUMBUS DAY: PAST FORMS OF VERBS

1. Words that show action or states of being are *verbs*. Verbs change to show time in the past.

basic form	past form		basic form	past form
is	was		give	gave
are	were		land	landed
live	lived		call	called
want	wanted		find	found
go	went		take	took
sail	sailed		know	knew
think	thought		buy	bought

2. Read the story again. Underline the past forms of the verbs.

3. a. Verbs that form the past by adding *-ed* are called regular verbs.

   b. Verbs that change in other ways are called irregular verbs.

4. Make two lists of verbs:

Regular Verbs

live	lived
____	____
____	____
____	____
____	____
____	____

Irregular Verbs

is	was
____	____
____	____
____	____
____	____
____	____

5. Verbs are words that show _____ or states of _____.

COLUMBUS DAY: QUESTION AND ANSWER FORMS IN THE PAST

1. a. Did Native Americans live in Spain?

   (DID + BASIC form of the verb)

   b. No, Native Americans didn't live in Spain.

   (DIDN'T + BASIC form of the verb)

   c. They lived in America.

2. a. In 1492, did people in Europe buy cars from the Indies?

   b. No, people in Europe didn't buy cars from the Indies.

   c. They bought perfume, spices, silk, and gold from the Indies.

3. a. Did Columbus want to go to the Indies by land?

   b. *No,* _____

   c. _____

4. a. Did Queen Isabella think Columbus was wrong?

   b. _____

   c. _____

5. a. Did Queen Isabella give Columbus five ships?

   b. _____

   c. _____

6. a. Did Columbus sail east?

   b. _____

   c. _____

7. a. Did Columbus discover the Indies?

   b. _____

   c. _____

COLUMBUS DAY MAZE

Help Columbus find the Indies.

THE DISCOVERY OF AMERICA

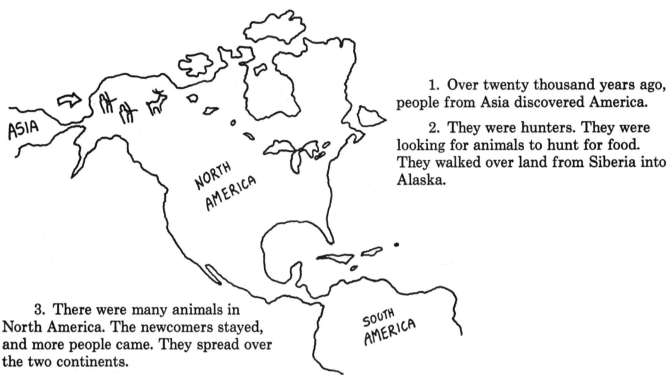

1. Over twenty thousand years ago, people from Asia discovered America.

2. They were hunters. They were looking for animals to hunt for food. They walked over land from Siberia into Alaska.

3. There were many animals in North America. The newcomers stayed, and more people came. They spread over the two continents.

4. After thousands of years, there were many different groups of people living in North and South America. They spoke different languages and had different ways of living.

5. Today, we call these people Native Americans.

6. Some of these Native Americans hunted animals and ate wild plants. Other Native Americans became farmers. In Mexico and South America, Native Americans built cities and great civilizations.

7. For thousands of years, the people in Europe did not know about America.

THE DISCOVERY OF AMERICA (continued)

8. In the year 600 A.D., Irish sailors sailed to America. They did not stay, and they did not bring others with them.

9. Bjarni Herjolfsson (Byárnee Hériúlfson) was a Viking. He sailed to the coast of America. He did not land. He told stories about the land he saw. This was in 986 A.D.

10. Leif Eriksson (Leef Ériksin), a Viking, heard the stories. He came to America a few years later. He called the land Vinland. The Vikings stayed in America for a short time.

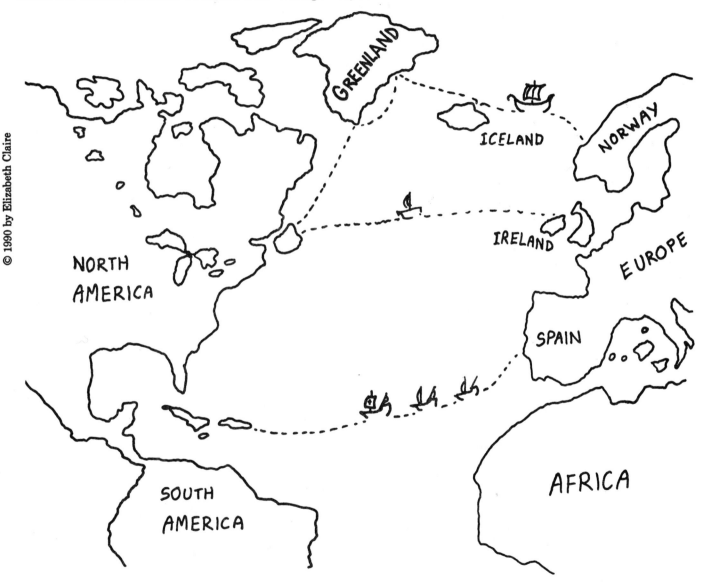

11. In 1492, Christopher Columbus came to America. He was Italian, but he was sailing in Spanish ships. He was looking for a way to go to Asia.

12. Columbus made four trips to America. He brought many people after him. But Christopher Columbus did not know that he had discovered a new continent.

THE DISCOVERY OF AMERICA: EXERCISES

I. Do you know these words? Draw a line under them in the story. Copy the words. Write the meanings.

thousand	spread	coast
ago	continent	Viking
Asia	language	hear/heard
discover	Native American	Italian
hunter	wild	Spanish
Siberia	civilization	bring/brought
newcomer	Irish	trip
stay	sailor	

II. What happened first? Write number 1 on the line in front of it. What happened next? Write number 2, then 3, 4, 5, and 6. The first one is done for you.

_____ Leif Eiriksson discovered America.

___1___ People from Asia discovered America.

_____ Christopher Columbus discovered America.

_____ The Irish discovered America.

_____ Bjarni Herjolfsson discovered America.

_____ I discovered America.

III. TRUE or FALSE?

___True___ 1. Many different groups of Native Americans lived in America.

_____ 2. Leif Eiriksson and Bjarni Herjolfsson were Vikings.

_____ 3. Irish sailors called America *Vinland*.

_____ 4. Christopher Columbus was Spanish, but he sailed in Italian ships.

_____ 5. Christopher Columbus knew that he had discovered a new continent.

CHRISTOPHER COLUMBUS

1. Christopher Columbus was born in Genoa, Italy in 1451. He loved the sea. He became a sailor when he was fifteen years old.

2. After many years and many travels, Columbus became an excellent sea captain. [He had many maps that showed that the earth was round. The maps showed that it was possible to sail west to get to the East.]

3. Columbus's maps showed that Japan was across the Atlantic Ocean, 2,700 miles away. Columbus did not know that his maps were wrong. Japan is really 12,200 miles to the west! And North and South America are in the way.

4. Columbus asked King Henry of Portugal for ships and sailors to discover the way to China and Japan. King Henry said no.

5. Then Columbus went to Spain and asked Queen Isabella and King Ferdinand. There was a war in Spain. "Wait until the war is over," Queen Isabella said.

6. Columbus had to wait many years. The war was over, at last, in 1492. Then Queen Isabella said yes.

7. The city of Palos gave Columbus three ships: the Niña, the Piñta, and the Santa Maria. Queen Isabella gave Columbus money and ninety sailors.

8. The three little ships sailed from Palos on August 3. First they stopped at the Canary Islands for more food and water. They left the Canaries on September 6.

9. The weather was good and the trip was easy. Columbus promised the sailors that they would all become rich. At first the sailors were excited. But day after day passed and they did not see land. The sailors became afraid.

10. After four weeks the sailors wanted to go back. They thought they would die if they didn't turn around.

11. Columbus said, "If we don't find land in three days, we will go back." He offered a prize to the first man to see land. Two times someone shouted, "Land!" but it was a mistake.

12. At last, they saw some birds. They followed the birds. On the thirty-fifth day, two hours after midnight, a sailor on the Pinta shouted "Land!" He could see land by the light of the moon.

13. That morning, October 12, all the men went ashore. They were very happy to be on land. They kissed the sand on the beach.

14. The people who lived on the island were the Arawak. They called their island Guahanal.

15. The Arawaks came to see the large ships and the sailors. They were amazed at the sailors' strange clothes. They were amazed at the beards on the sailors' faces.

16. The Arawaks thought the ships and the men had sailed down from the sky. They brought the sailors presents, food, and parrots.

CHRISTOPHER COLUMBUS (continued)

17. Columbus and his men gave presents to the Arawaks, too. He tried to ask them if this island was part of Japan. They could only use sign language. Columbus thought that he was in the Indies. He called the people Indians.

18. Columbus named the island San Salvador. He claimed San Salvador for the King and Queen of Spain. He did not ask the Arawaks if they would like to belong to Spain.

19. Columbus sailed to other islands. He left forty sailors on the island of Hispaniola. He returned home to Spain with just two ships. He took home many things to show Queen Isabella. He brought parrots, pearls, gold, and six "Indians."

20. When the two little ships returned, the people in Spain were very, very excited. As the ships came into the port of Palos, cannons thundered, church bells clanged, and people cheered.

21. Queen Isabella made Columbus the ruler of the lands he discovered. She was very happy with his discoveries.

22. Many sailors wanted to go with Columbus on his next trip. They thought they would find gold and become rich. The next year Columbus sailed again. This time he had seventeen ships and fifteen hundred men.

23. He sailed to other islands, and to Honduras, the coast of Florida, Venezuela, and Panama.

24. The men who went with him did not find a lot of gold. They were disappointed. Some of them said Columbus was a cruel leader. They sent him to jail in Spain.

25. Isabella freed Columbus, and he went back to Hispaniola. He lived there for ten years. He was rich, but he was not healthy. He went back to Spain where he died in 1506.

26. Americans remember Columbus in many ways. Places are named for him, such as the District of Columbia; Columbus, Ohio; and Columbia, South Carolina. Columbia is a nickname for the United States in several songs. Columbia University is named for Columbus. Hundreds of schools are named for him. There is a famous statue of Columbus at Columbus Circle in New York.

27. Americans celebrate Columbus Day with parades, parties, and good times. The year 1992 is the five hundredth anniversary of Columbus's discovery of America.

UNITED NATIONS DAY

1. October 24 is the birthday of the United Nations.

2. The UN began in 1945. In 1989, 159 countries were members of the UN.

3. The United Nations was formed to keep peace in the world. Countries can discuss their disagreements without going to war.

4. The UN has other purposes too. The UN works to prevent famine.

5. The UN works to fight disease.

INOCULATIONS

TRAIN DOCTORS

CLEAN WATER

6. The UN works to decrease poverty.

LAND REFORM   LOANS to FARMERS

7. The UN works to increase literacy.

SCHOOLS

BOOKS

TEACHERS

8. The UN works to protect human rights.

FREEDOM   DIGNITY

EQUALITY

JUSTICE

UNITED NATIONS DAY (continued)

9. The UN helps people when there is an earthquake, flood, or other disaster.

10. The United Nations meets in the UN Building at Forty-second Street in New York City.

11. There is a World Court, too. The World Court is in The Hague, Netherlands.

12. The Security Council is part of the UN. There are five permanent members: the United States, Great Britain, France, China, and the Soviet Union. The General Assembly elects ten other members.

13. The General Assembly has 159 members.

14. There are six official languages of the UN: English, French, Spanish, Russian, Chinese, and Arabic.

UNITED NATIONS DAY: EXERCISES

I. Do you know these words? Find the words in the story. Draw a line under them. Copy the words. Write the meanings.

united	purpose	rights
nations	prevent	earthquake
begin/began	famine	flood
member	decrease	disaster
form	disease	court
peace	poverty	the Netherlands
world	increase	Security Council
discuss	literacy	permanent
disagreement	protect	General Assembly
war	human	elect
	official	

II. Complete the sentences. Answer the questions.

1. United Nations Day is _____.

2. Today, there are _____ countries in the UN.

3. The UN was formed to _____.

4. Other purposes of the UN are:

    a. _____

    b. _____

    c. _____

    d. _____

5. Where does the UN meet? _____

6. How many members are in the Security Council? _____

7. What countries are the five permanent members?

_____

_____

8. What are the six official languages of the UN?

_____

_____

9. What is the official language of your native country? _____

UNITED NATIONS DAY: EXERCISES *(continued)*

10. What languages can you speak? _____

11. What problems does the world have today? _____

_____

_____

III. Copy the information below and then fill in the missing words.

COUNTRY	NATIONALITY	LANGUAGE
1. United States	American	English
2. Canada	Canadian	English and French
3. Israel	Israeli	Hebrew
4. Spain	Spanish	Spanish
5. Colombia	_____	_____
6. France	_____	_____
7. Italy	_____	_____
8. Japan	_____	_____
9. Korea	_____	_____
10. China	_____	_____
11. Soviet Union	_____	_____
12. Great Britain	_____	_____
13. Mexico	_____	_____
14. Brazil	_____	_____
15. Vietnam	_____	_____
16. Iran	_____	_____
17. Saudi Arabia	_____	_____
18. _____	_____	_____
19. _____	_____	_____
20. _____	_____	_____

IV. ACTIVITIES
1. Draw a map of your native country.
2. Draw the flag of your native country.
3. Play "UN Bingo" with the names of twenty-four countries.

Name _____   Date _____

STANDARD TIME

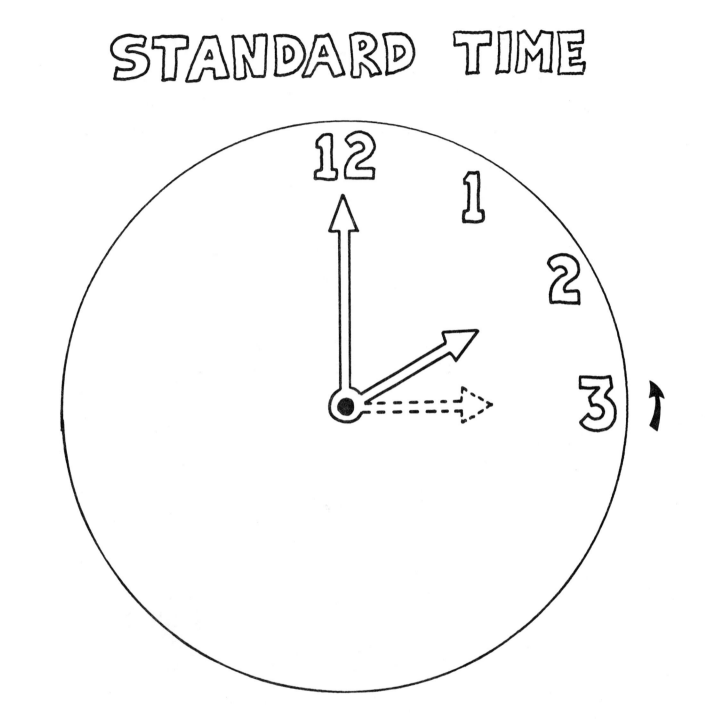

On Sunday, October _____, we turn back the clock one hour. We will return to _____
Standard Time. The official time goes back at 3:00 A.M. Sunday morning.

HALLOWEEN

HALLOWEEN: VOCABULARY BUILDING

I. Can you find these things in the picture?

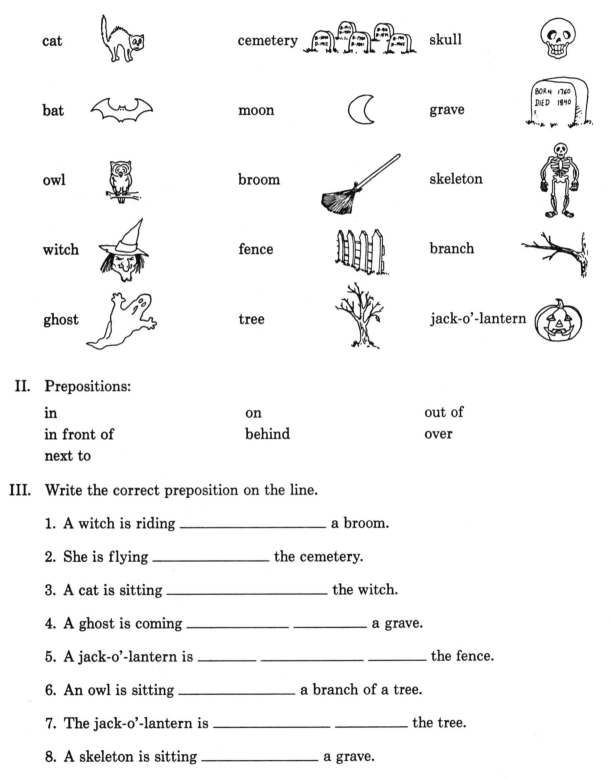

cat

bat

owl

witch

ghost

cemetery

moon

broom

fence

tree

skull

grave

skeleton

branch

jack-o'-lantern

II. Prepositions:

in	on	out of
in front of	behind	over
next to		

III. Write the correct preposition on the line.

1. A witch is riding _____ a broom.

2. She is flying _____ the cemetery.

3. A cat is sitting _____ the witch.

4. A ghost is coming _____ _____ a grave.

5. A jack-o'-lantern is _____ _____ _____ the fence.

6. An owl is sitting _____ a branch of a tree.

7. The jack-o'-lantern is _____ _____ the tree.

8. A skeleton is sitting _____ a grave.

TRICK OR TREAT

1. October 31 is Halloween.

2. Children like Halloween.

3. Children wear costumes and masks.

4. They go to their neighbors' houses.

5. They knock on the door.

6. They say, "Trick or Treat!"

7. The neighbor gives them candy or money.

8. The children say, "Thank you."

TRICK OR TREAT: EXERCISES

I. Do you know these words? Find the words in the story. Draw a line under them. Copy the words. Write the meanings.

October	mask	give/gave
children	neighbors'	candy
like	knock	money
wear/wore	say/said	thank you
costume	trick or treat	Halloween

II. Write the correct words on the lines:

October 31 is _____. Children _____ Halloween.

Children _____ costumes and masks. They go to their _____

houses. The children _____ on the door. They say, "_____!"

The neighbor gives them _____ or _____. The children

say _____ _____."

III. Write the plural form for these words:

Singular   *Plural*

a. costume   _____

b. mask   _____

c. apple   _____

d. pumpkin   _____

e. door   _____

f. neighbor   _____

g. child   _____

HALLOWEEN COSTUMES: VOCABULARY BUILDING

I. Do you know these words? Find the words in the story. Draw a line under them. Copy the words. Write the meanings.

some	buy/bought	sometimes
funny	make/made	prize
beautiful	wear/wore	best
ugly	parade	

II. Match:

1. clown _____   A

2. princess _____   B

3. monster _____   C

4. hobo _____   D

5. devil _____   E

6. rabbit _____   F

7. pumpkin _____   G

8. cowboy _____   H

Name _____   Date _____

HALLOWEEN SAFETY

1. Choose a safe mask. You need to see. You need to breathe.

2. Choose a safe costume. You need to walk. You need to sit.

3. Go to your friends' and neighbors' houses. Do not go to strangers' houses.

4. Be careful when you cross the street.

5. Do not go "trick or treating" alone. Go with your friends.

6. Take all of the treats home. Look at them very carefully.

7. Do not eat too much candy!

HALLOWEEN SAFETY: VOCABULARY BUILDING

I. Do you know these words? Find the words in the story. Draw a line under them. Copy the words. Write the meanings.

safety	breathe	friend
safe	stranger	treats
choose	be careful	home
need	cross	too much
see/saw	alone	

II. Complete the sentences:

1. Choose a _____ mask. You _____ to see.

2. Choose a _____ costume. You need to _____.

3. You need to _____. You need to _____.

4. Go to the home of a neighbor or _____.

5. Don't go to the home of a _____.

6. Be careful when you _____ the street.

7. Do not go trick or treating _____.

8. Look at the _____ very carefully before you eat them.

9. Do not eat _____ candy.

HOW TO MAKE A JACK-O'-LANTERN

1. Buy a nice orange pumpkin.

2. Wash the pumpkin.

3. Put newspapers on the table.

4. Cut a large hole around the top. Use a sharp knife. Be careful.

5. Take out the seeds.

6. Cut out eyes, a nose, and a mouth.

7. Put a candle in the pumpkin.

8. Put the top on. Turn off the lights. Now you have a jack-o'-lantern! Ahhhh!

HOW TO MAKE A JACK-O'-LANTERN: EXERCISES

I. Do you know these words? Find the words in the story. Draw a line under them. Copy the words. Write the meanings.

pumpkin	be careful	seed
wash	top	candle
newspaper	sharp	around
cut	knife	light
hole	take out/took out	

II. How do you make a jack-o'-lantern? What comes first? Write 1. What comes next? Write 2. Then write 3, 4, 5, 6, 7, and 8.

_____ Cut out eyes, a nose and a mouth.

_____ Wash the pumpkin.

___1___ Buy a nice orange pumpkin.

_____ Cut a large hole around the top of the pumpkin.

_____ Put newspapers on the table.

_____ Take out the seeds.

_____ Turn off the lights.

_____ Put the top on the pumpkin.

III. Draw a happy pumpkin, a sad pumpkin, and a scary pumpkin.

A HALLOWEEN GAME

1. Fill a big tub with water.

2. Put apples in the water.

3. Get down on your knees.

4. Put your hands behind your back.

5. Open your mouth. Try to get an apple. Good luck!

6. This is called "bobbing for apples."

7. Now you need a towel.

8. You can eat the apple. Mmmmm. Delicious.

ELECTION DAY

Americans vote for their leaders on Election Day.

Name _____ Date _____

ALL ABOUT ELECTION DAY

1. Election Day is in November. It is the first Tuesday after the first Monday.

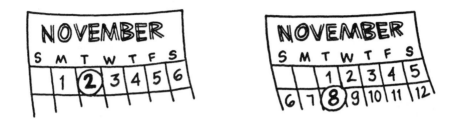

2. On this day, Americans elect leaders for their cities, states, and nation. Every four years, Americans elect a president and vice president.

3. For many months before Election Day, there is a campaign. The candidates visit many different places. They make speeches. They advertise on radio and TV.

4. Citizens eighteen years old and over may vote. No one can know how another person votes. There is a secret ballot.

5. The voter walks into the voting booth. A curtain closes. The voter votes for the candidates he or she likes. When the voter is finished, the machine counts the vote. The curtain opens.

6. The polls close in the evening. The counting begins.

7. It takes a few days to add all the votes. But computers can often tell the winner after a few hours.

ELECTION DAY: EXERCISES

I. Do you know these words? Find the words in the story. Draw a line under them. Copy the words. Write the meanings.

elect	citizen	secret
election	campaign	voting booth
city	candidate	polls
state	visit	computer
nation	speech	winner
president	advertise	four
vice president	vote	eighteen

II. Complete the sentences.

1. _____ Day is the first Tuesday after the first Monday in November.

2. Every _____ years, Americans elect a president and vice president.

3. Citizens _____ years old or over may vote.

4. Americans vote with a _____ ballot.

5. Candidates make speeches. They _____ on TV and radio.

GENERAL ELECTION SAMPLE BALLOT

PERSONAL CHOICE		DEMOCRAT COLUMN 1	REPUBLICAN COLUMN 2	OTHER COLUMN 3	QUESTION COLUMN	PUBLIC QUESTIONS
	PRESIDENT VICE-PRESIDENT					PUBLIC QUESTION NO. 1
	U.S. SENATOR					
	U.S. HOUSE OF REPRESENTATIVES				YES NO	
	GOVERNOR LIEUT. GOVERNOR					PUBLIC QUESTION NO. 2
	MEMBERS OF GENERAL ASSEMBLY (VOTE FOR TWO)				YES NO	
	STATE SENATOR					AMENDMENT TO THE STATE CONSTITUTION
	MEMBERS OF THE COUNTY BOARD (VOTE FOR TWO)					
	MAYOR (VOTE FOR ONE)				YES NO	
	MEMBERS OF THE TOWN COUNCIL (VOTE FOR THREE)					

Name _____   Date _____

LET'S TALK ABOUT ELECTION DAY

DO YOU KNOW. . . .

1. Who is the president of the United States now? _____

2. Who is the vice president? _____

3. Who is the governor of your state? _____

4. Who is the mayor of your town or city? _____

5. Who is the principal of your school? _____

6. Who are the candidates for office this year? _____

_____

7. What political parties are they from?

_____

_____

8. How often are elections for these offices?

_____

9. What day is Election Day? _____

10. Where can people in your neighborhood vote?

_____

11. Who is t[...] *P. 61, 62, 63* _____
    5 copies each

12. Is he or [...] _____

13. How often are elections for this o[...]? _____

VETERANS DAY

TOMB OF THE UNKNOWN SOLDIER

November 11 is Veterans Day. A veteran is a soldier or other person who served in the United States Armed Services.

Many people served and fought in wars for the United States. We remember these soldiers and other veterans on Veterans Day.

Name _____ Date _____

THE STORY OF VETERANS DAY

1. November 11 is Veterans Day. A veteran is a soldier who has fought in a war.

2. Thirty-five countries fought in World War I. They fought for five years, from 1914 to 1918. The United States was in the war from 1917 to 1918.

3. Finally the countries stopped fighting. The leaders signed an armistic (ár mə stis). They signed the armistice on the eleventh hour of the eleventh day of the eleventh month. The armistice meant that the war was over.

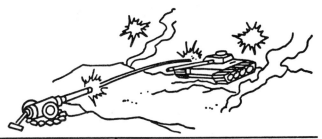

4. Americans were very happy to hear about the armistice. No more soldiers would die in the war. The soldiers could come home.

5. People went out into streets and laughed and danced. They blew horns and whistles and rang bells. They sang songs. They thought that there would never be another war.

THE STORY OF VETERANS DAY (continued)

6. President Wilson made November 11 a holiday to remember the end of the war. The holiday was called Armistice Day.

7. At eleven o'clock in the morning, everyone stopped doing whatever they were doing. People were completely silent for one minute. This minute was to remember all the soldiers who have died in wars.

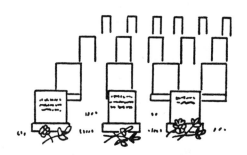

8. The body of an unknown soldier was brought to America from the cemetery in France. His body was buried in a tomb at Arlington National Cemetery. It was called the Tomb of the Unknown Soldier.

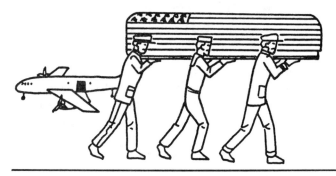

9. The US was in three more wars, World War II, the Korean War, and the Vietnam War. The name of the holiday was changed to Veterans Day.

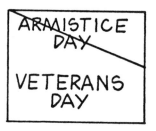

10. The bodies of three more unknown soldiers were brought to the cemetery. On Veterans Day, there are special services at the Tomb of the Unknowns.

11. Americans remember and honor all the veterans who fought in wars.

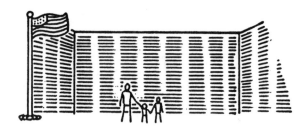

© 1990 by Elizabeth Claire

© 1990 by Elizabeth Claire

VETERANS DAY: EXERCISES

I. Do you know these words? Find the words in the story. Draw a line under them. Copy the words. Write the meanings.

veteran	horn	honor
soldiers	whistle	unknown
fight/fought	ring/rang	war
world war	bell	eleven
country	silent	tomb
armistice	silence	remember
leader	bury	services
sign	cemetery	

II. Complete the sentences and answer the questions.

1. The armistice meant that the _____ was over.

2. On Veterans Day we honor the _____ who fought in the wars.

3. At _____ o'clock on November 11, there is one minute of silence.

4. Do you have a day to remember soldiers who died in wars? _____

5. When is it? _____

6. What happens on that day? _____

_____

7. What are the reasons that nations go to war?

_____

_____

_____

8. Are there better ways to solve problems between nations?

_____

_____

_____

_____

PUERTO RICAN DISCOVERY DAY

1. Christopher Columbus made four trips to America. On the second trip, he discovered a beautiful island. He named it San Juan Bautista. The day was November 19, 1493. This day is called Puerto Rican Discovery Day.

2. The people who lived on this island were Arawaks. The Arawaks were farmers. They called their island Borinquen, "Land of the Brave Lord." The Arawaks were very friendly to Columbus.

3. The Spanish built a capital city near the sea. They named it Puerto Rico, or "Rich Port." Later, the name of the island (San Juan) became the name of the capital, and the name of the capital city became the name of the island.

4. In Puerto Rico and in New York City there are big parades with music, costumes, and fun on Puerto Rican Discovery Day. It is also called "Dia de la Raza."

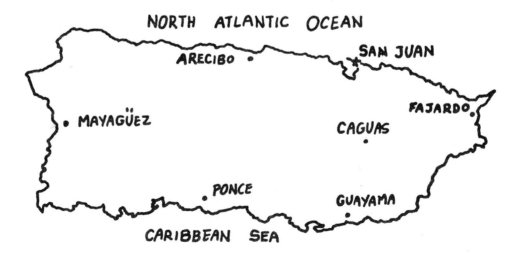

PUERTO RICAN DISCOVERY DAY: EXERCISES

I. Do you know these words? Find these words in the story. Draw a line under them. Copy the words. Write the meanings of the words.

trip	brave	city
second	lord	sea
discover	friendly	port
discovery	Spanish	parade
island	build/built	music
farmer	capital	costume
		fun

II. Yes or No?

1. Columbus made six trips to America. _____

2. On the second trip he discovered a beautiful island. _____

3. He named the island Borinquen. _____

4. The people on the island were Arawak. _____

5. The Arawak were farmers. _____

6. The Arawak built a capital city near the sea. _____

7. Puerto Rico means "Rich Port." _____

8. Today, the name of the city is San Juan, and the name of the island is Puerto Rico.

_____

9. In Puerto Rico and New York City there are parades on Puerto Rican Discovery Day.

_____

10. Another name for this day is "Dia de la Raza." _____

Name _____   Date _____

THE FLAG OF PUERTO RICO

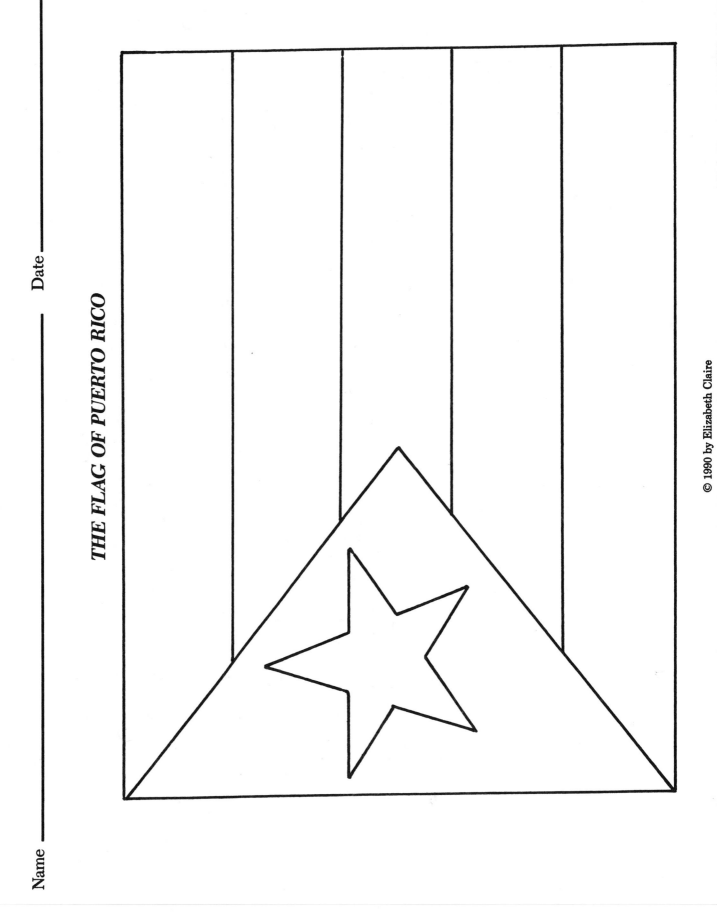

Thanksgiving Day is a day to give thanks for the things we have.

Name _____ Date _____

ALL ABOUT THANKSGIVING

1. The fourth Thursday of November is Thanksgiving.

2. This year, Thanksgiving is November

_____.

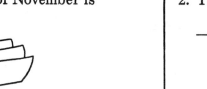

3. There is no school on Thanksgiving. There is no school on Friday.

4. Thanksgiving is a happy holiday.

5. Families get together on Thanksgiving. They invite friends too.

6. Americans like to eat a big dinner on Thanksgiving. Most people eat turkey.

7. Other traditional foods are corn, stuffing, beans, sweet potatoes, gravy, and cranberry sauce.

8. Traditional desserts are apple pie and pumpkin pie.

© 1990 by Elizabeth Claire

THANKSGIVING: EXERCISES

I. Do you know these words? Find the words in the story. Draw a line under them. Copy the words. Write the meanings.

fourth	invite	corn
Thursday	friends	stuffing
November	eat/ate	sweet potatoes
Thanksgiving	dinner	beans
year	traditional	cranberry sauce
families	turkey	pie
get together		

II. Complete the sentences:

1. The fourth Thursday of _____ is Thanksgiving.

2. _____ get together on Thanksgiving.

3. Most people eat _____ on Thanksgiving.

4. Match:

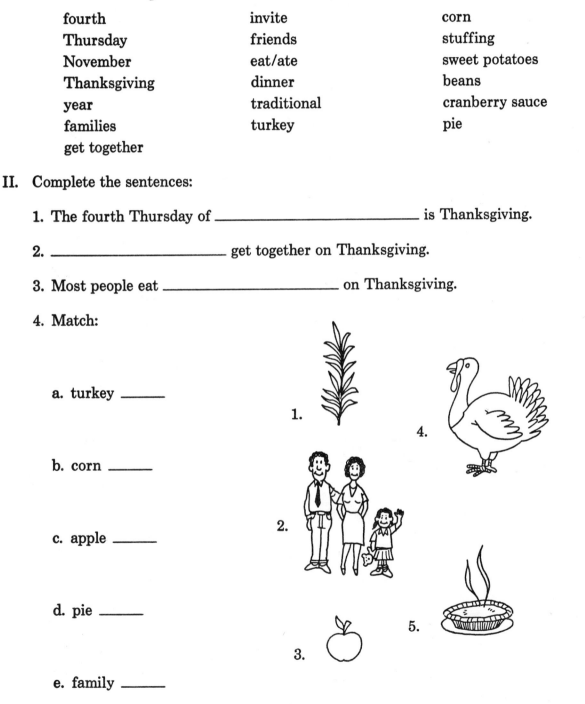

a. turkey _____

b. corn _____

c. apple _____

d. pie _____

e. family _____

Name —————————————————————— Date ——————————

WHAT ARE YOU THANKFUL FOR THIS YEAR?

—————————————————————————————————————

—————————————————————————————————————

—————————————————————————————————————

—————————————————————————————————————

—————————————————————————————————————

—————————————————————————————————————

—————————————————————————————————————

—————————————————————————————————————

Draw pictures of what you are thankful for. Write sentences that begin with "I am thankful for . . ."
or "I am thankful that . . ."

THE STORY OF THANKSGIVING

1. In the year 1620, a little ship came to America. It was called the Mayflower. There were one hundred people on the ship.

2. The people were called Pilgrims. They came from England.

3. The Pilgrims wanted to have their own church. They could not have their own church in England.

4. The first winter in America was very cold. The Pilgrims did not have much food. They did not have warm clothes.

WE'RE HUNGRY!

5. The Pilgrims got sick. Many Pilgrims died. It was a terrible time.

6. In the spring, Indians came to visit. They were friendly. Two Indians could speak English!

HELLO!

THE STORY OF THANKSGIVING (continued)

7. The Indians showed the Pilgrims how to plant corn.

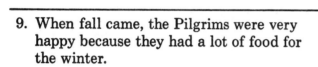

8. The Pilgrims worked hard. They cut down trees. They built houses. They learned to hunt the turkeys that lived in the woods.

9. When fall came, the Pilgrims were very happy because they had a lot of food for the winter.

10. They made a big dinner. They invited the Indians to come and eat with them.

11. The Indians brought deer for the dinner. They cooked outside. They ate and ate for three days.

12. The Pilgrims were thankful for the good things they had. This was the first Thanksgiving in America.

THE STORY OF THANKSGIVING: EXERCISES

I. Do you know these words? Find these words in the story. Draw a line under them. Copy the words. Write the meanings.

ship	die	learn
people	terrible	hunt
Pilgrims	spring	turkey
England	Indian	woods
church	show	fall
own	plant	winter
winter	corn	invite
food	work	bring/brought
warm	cut	outside
clothes	build/built	first
sick	trees	

II. Choose the correct answer:

1. The Pilgrims came to America by _____. (ship, jet, bus)

2. The name of the ship was _____. (Pilgrims, Indians, the Mayflower)

3. The Pilgrims came from _____. (America, England, Japan)

4. The first winter was very _____. (cold, warm, happy)

5. Many pilgrims got sick and _____. (went back to England, planted seeds, died)

6. The _____ brought food to the Pilgrims. (turkeys, Indians, seeds)

7. The Indians showed the Pilgrims how to plant _____. (grass, trees, corn)

8. When fall came, the Pilgrims were very happy because they had a lot of _____ for the winter. (Indians, trees, food)

9. The Pilgrims made a big dinner and invited the _____ to come and eat with them. (sick, Indians, farmers)

10. They gave _____ for the good things they had. (corn, thanks, gifts)

Name _____ Date _____

THE STORY OF THANKSGIVING: EXERCISES *(continued)*

III. Match

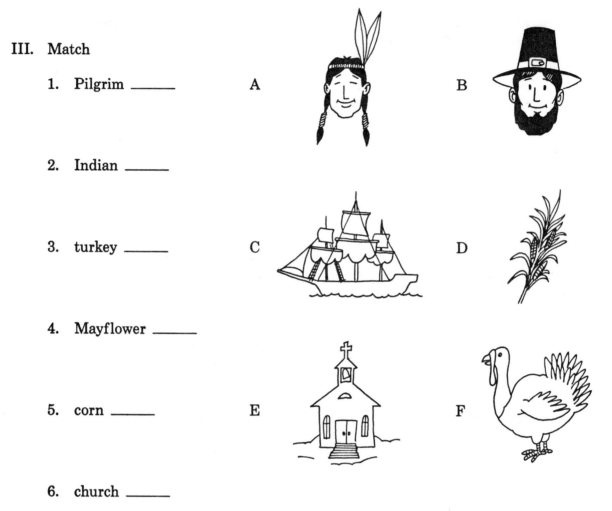

1. Pilgrim _____   A

2. Indian _____

3. turkey _____   C   D

4. Mayflower _____

5. corn _____   E   F

6. church _____

THANKSGIVING: PAST FORMS

I. 1. A verb is a word that shows action. Verbs change to show the past.

Basic Form	Affirmative Past Form
are	were
can	could
come	came
want	wanted
call	called
have	had
get	got
bring	brought
show	showed
work	worked
cut	cut
build	built
learn	learned
make	made
invite	invited
eat	ate
cook	cooked
give	gave

2. Verbs that show the past with *-ed* are called *regular verbs*.

3. Verbs that change in other ways are called *irregular verbs*.

II. Make two lists of verbs from the Thanksgiving story.

Regular verbs	Irregular verbs
_____	_____
_____	_____
_____	_____
_____	_____
_____	_____
_____	_____
_____	_____
_____	_____

THANKSGIVING: PAST FORMS (continued)

Answer in complete sentences.

1. Where did the Pilgrims come from?

   The Pilgrims came from England.

2. What did the Pilgrims want?

   _____

3. Did many Pilgrims die the first winter?

   _____

4. Who came to visit in the spring?

   _____

5. What did the Indians show the Pilgrims?

   _____

6. What did the Pilgrims build?

   _____

7. Whom did the Pilgrims invite to the Thanksgiving dinner?

   _____

8. What did the Indians bring to the dinner?

   _____

9. What else did they eat?

   _____

THANKSGIVING MATCH-UP AND VOCABULARY

I. Find the match. Write the letter on the line.

1. the Pilgrims' boat _____   A. home, family, and friends

2. the Pilgrims' friends _____   B. December, January, February

3. fall _____   C. fourth Thursday in November

4. winter _____   D. Indians

5. Thanksgiving dinner _____   E. the Mayflower

6. Thanksgiving Day _____   F. turkey, stuffing, potatoes, corn, beans, apple pie

7. woods _____   G. many trees

8. gravy _____   H. September, October, November

9. I am thankful for my _____   I. sauce for meat or turkey

II. Draw a circle around the word that does not belong with the other words in each line.

1. spring	fall	September	summer
2. October	Thursday	November	December
3. Pilgrims	Americans	England	Indians
4. holiday	corn	beans	pumpkin
5. Halloween	Mayflower	Thanksgiving	Columbus Day
6. cold	hot	happy	warm
7. king	church	school	house
8. train	boat	jet	water

TEACHER'S CHOICE:
THANKSGIVING WEEK ACTIVITIES

1. Have a tasting party. Have students learn the names of foods and adjectives to describe them. Include cranberry sauce, stuffing, pumpkin pie, and apples.

2. Prepare a snack, lunch, or full Thanksgiving meal. Invite other students or teachers to join you. Show students how to set the table American style and teach them the names for knife, fork, spoon, plate, glass, cup, pot, pitcher, and so on.

3. Make a class Thanksgiving collage on the bulletin board. Ask students to cut out pictures that represent the things they are thankful for, and use these pictures to make the collage.

4. Ask students to make "turkeys" using the following directions:

    a. Trace one hand on brown paper. Cut it out, then draw the beak, eyes, legs, and wattle on colored paper and cut out. Put the turkey together on another sheet of paper.

    b. Thread raisins on toothpicks. Stick them into a marshmallow to form tail feathers and a neck. A large grape can be used for the head.

5. Play "Thanksgiving Bingo."

HANUKKAH

Hanukkah is the Festival of Lights.

HANUKKAH: THE FESTIVAL OF LIGHTS

1. Hanukkah is in December. It lasts for eight days. This year, Hanukkah is December _____ to _____.

2. Hanukkah is a Jewish holiday. Another name for Hanukkah is "The Festival of Lights."

3. This is a menorah. On the first night of Hanukkah, the family lights one candle.

4. They say prayers and tell the story of Hanukkah.

5. On the second night, they light two candles.

6. On the third night, they light three candles, and so on for eight days.

7. Families eat a big dinner. They sing songs.

8. Children play a game with a dreidel. Some families give money and gifts to children on Hanukkah.

HANUKKAH: EXERCISES

I. Do you know these words? Find the words in the story. Draw a line under the words. Copy the words. Write the meanings.

Hanukkah	candle	sing
December	say prayers	song
to last for 8 days	story	children
Jewish	second	game
festival	third	dreidel
menorah	and so on	money
light/lit	family	gift

II.   NUMBERS

Cardinal		*Ordinal*	
one	1	first	1st
two	2	second	2nd
three	3	third	3rd
four	4	fourth	4th
five	5	fifth	5th
six	6	sixth	6th
seven	7	seventh	7th
eight	8	eighth	8th
nine	9	ninth	9th
ten	10	tenth	10th
twenty-one	21	twenty-first	21st
thirty-one	31	thirty-first	31st

III. Yes or No?

1. Hanukkah is the Festival of Lights. _____

2. On the first night of Hanukkah, Jews light three candles. _____

3. On the fourth night, Jews light four candles. _____

4. Families get together on Hanukkah. _____

5. Children play a game with a dreidel. _____

6. Some families give turkeys to children on Hanukkah. _____

THE STORY OF HANUKKAH

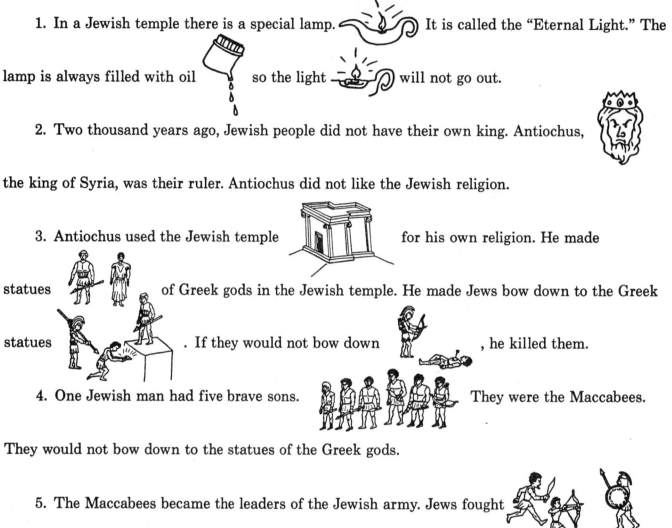

1. In a Jewish temple there is a special lamp. It is called the "Eternal Light." The lamp is always filled with oil so the light will not go out.

2. Two thousand years ago, Jewish people did not have their own king. Antiochus, the king of Syria, was their ruler. Antiochus did not like the Jewish religion.

3. Antiochus used the Jewish temple for his own religion. He made statues of Greek gods in the Jewish temple. He made Jews bow down to the Greek statues. If they would not bow down, he killed them.

4. One Jewish man had five brave sons. They were the Maccabees. They would not bow down to the statues of the Greek gods.

5. The Maccabees became the leaders of the Jewish army. Jews fought against Antiochus and his armies. They got the Temple back. But the Eternal Light was out.

6. The Jews lit the Eternal Light. They had only enough oil for one day. They had to get more oil. It took eight days to get more oil. But a miracle happened. The light did not go out after one day. It burned for eight days until the new oil was ready .

7. Since that day, Jews have celebrated the "Miracle of the Lights," or Hanukkah, every year.

Name _____ Date _____

THE STORY OF HANUKKAH: EXERCISES

I. Do you know these words? Draw a line under the words in the story. Copy the words. Write the meanings.

temple	religion	leader
lamp	own	army
eternal	statues	fight/fought
filled	Greek	light/lit
oil	god	enough
go out/went out	bow down	miracle
thousand	kill	burn
king	brave	since
ruler	son	celebrate

II. MATCH:

1. The Eternal Light _____   A. King of Syria

2. Antiochus _____   B. Hanukkah

3. the Maccabees _____   C. leaders of the Jewish army

4. The Festival of Lights _____   D. never goes out

III. True or False?

1. Antiochus was a good king for the Jews. _____

2. The Jews wanted to bow down to Greek gods. _____

3. The Maccabees were brave Jews. _____

4. When the Jews got the Temple back, the Eternal Light was out. _____

5. They had oil for only one day. _____

6. The oil burned for six days. _____

THE DREIDEL GAME

1. You can play the dreidel game. A dreidel is a top that has four sides. Each side has a letter from the Hebrew alphabet.

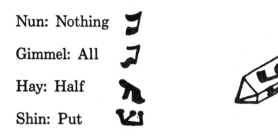

Nun: Nothing ‎נ

Gimmel: All ‎ג

Hay: Half ‎ה

Shin: Put ‎ש

2. The letters stand for a Hebrew sentence: "Nes gadol haya sham." It means, "A great miracle happened there."

3. The players have buttons, candies, or pennies. Each player puts one button, candy, or penny into a pot in the center of the table.

4. Spin the dreidel.

   a. If the side up is nun, do nothing.

   b. If it is gimmel, take all of the things in the pot.

   c. If it is hay, take half.

   d. If it is shin, put one in the pot.

The Dreidel Song

I have a little dreidel,
I made it out of clay.
And when it's dry and ready,
Then dreidel I shall play.

O dreidel, dreidel, dreidel,
I made it out of clay.
And when it's dry and ready,
With dreidel I shall play.

It has a lovely body
With legs so short and thin,
And when it gets all tired
It drops and then I win.

My dreidel's always playful,
It loves to dance and spin.
A happy game of dreidel
Come play now let's begin.

O dreidel, dreidel, dreidel!
It loves to dance and spin.
O dreidel, dreidel, dreidel!
Come play now let's begin.

Winter begins December 21. In some parts of the United States it is cold in winter. It snows. Some **animals sleep all winter.**

WINTER: EXERCISES

I. Can you find these things in the picture?

snow	snowsuit	hat
snowman	icicles	tree
snowball	boots	squirrel
snow fort	scarf	groundhog
snow shovel	coat	mittens

II. Read the sentences below. Underline each word from the list above.

1. A child is making a snowman.

2. A boy is shoveling snow.

3. A boy is throwing a snowball.

4. There is a snow fort in front of the house.

5. There are snowballs next to the snow fort.

6. A squirrel is on the tree.

7. There are icicles on the house.

8. The boy and girl are wearing mittens.

9. The snowman has a scarf around its neck.

10. The groundhog is sleeping.

TEACHER'S CHOICE: MAKE A SNOWFLAKE

Distribute squares of white paper. You can let students make squares from 8½-by-11-inch paper instead if you wish.

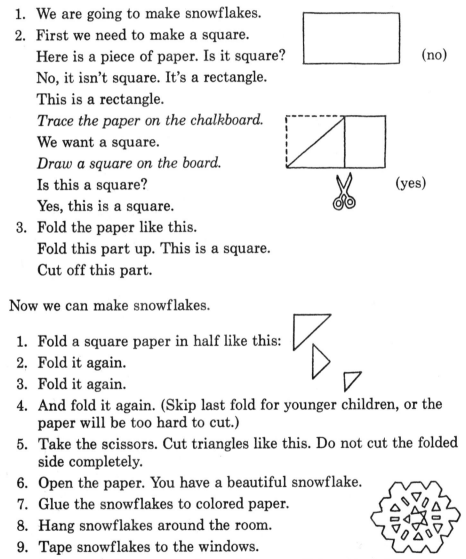

1. We are going to make snowflakes.
2. First we need to make a square.
   Here is a piece of paper. Is it square? (no)
   No, it isn't square. It's a rectangle.
   This is a rectangle.
   Trace the paper on the chalkboard.
   We want a square.
   Draw a square on the board.
   Is this a square? (yes)
   Yes, this is a square.
3. Fold the paper like this.
   Fold this part up. This is a square.
   Cut off this part.

Now we can make snowflakes.

1. Fold a square paper in half like this:
2. Fold it again.
3. Fold it again.
4. And fold it again. (Skip last fold for younger children, or the paper will be too hard to cut.)
5. Take the scissors. Cut triangles like this. Do not cut the folded side completely.
6. Open the paper. You have a beautiful snowflake.
7. Glue the snowflakes to colored paper.
8. Hang snowflakes around the room.
9. Tape snowflakes to the windows.
10. Dab some glue on the edges of the snowflakes. Sprinkle on some glitter. Let it dry. Then shake off excess glitter.
11. Make a snowflake out of aluminum foil. Then paste it on blue or black paper.
12. Make small snowflakes and paste them on folded paper to make greeting cards.

TEACHER'S CHOICE:
THE HOLIDAY PROJECT

You and your students are invited to participate in the Holiday Project. The Holiday Project is a network of volunteers who visit people in nursing homes, hospitals, and institutions during the Hanukkah and Christmas season. The visitors distribute small gifts. They sing holiday songs and invite the patients to sing along. It is a delightful way to experience the true meaning of the holidays.

The gifts are donated by businesses and individuals.

You can choose to participate in a variety of ways:

1. Visit a facility near you with others on Hanukkah or Christmas; sing, ring jingle bells, distribute gifts, smile. Invite students and their parents to come. Practice singing Christmas carols and Hanukkah songs in advance. (Check with your local organizer for dates, times, and appropriate songs to learn.)

2. Volunteer to organize and lead a group of ten to twenty people to a facility near you. Training and guidance are provided.

3. Collect donations and small gifts from stores, companies, and individuals.

4. Attend a gift-wrapping party about a week before the holidays.

Write the following address for the name of a Holiday Project coordinator near you.

Holiday Project, Central Office
P.O. Box 6829
FDR Station
New York, New York 10150-1906

Name _____

Date _____

CHRISTMAS

Can you find these things in the picture: fireplace, tree, decorations, gifts, stockings, toys, Santa Claus, wreath, candle, mistletoe, cards, candy canes, poinsettia?

GETTING READY FOR CHRISTMAS

1. December 25 is Christmas. Christmas is a Christian holiday. Many other people enjoy Christmas too.

2. People decorate their homes.

3. They decorate Christmas trees.

4. People make or buy gifts for their family and friends.

5. People send Christmas cards.

6. It is a time to remember poor people too.

7. Many people bake cookies for Christmas.

8. Children visit Santa Claus in stores. Other children write letters to him.

© 1990 by Elizabeth Claire

Name _____ Date _____

GETTING READY FOR CHRISTMAS (continued)

9. People sing Christmas carols. They sing carols in the street, in hospitals, and in nursing homes.

SILENT NIGHT ♫
♫ HOLY NIGHT

10. People tell Christmas stories.

'TWAS THE NIGHT BEFORE CHRISTMAS...

11. On Christmas Eve, many people go to church.

12. Children hang up stockings. They hope that Santa Claus will fill the stockings with toys.

13. Families and friends have Christmas parties and dinners.

14. People give gifts to each other.

FOR YOU

OH THANKS

GETTING READY FOR CHRISTMAS: EXERCISES

I. Do you know these words? Find these words in the story. Draw a line under them. Copy the words. Write the meanings.

Christmas	remember	story/stories
December	poor	Christmas Eve
Christian	bake	church
enjoy	cookies	hang up/hung up
decorate	visit	stockings
homes	Santa Claus	hope
tree	stores	fill
gift	write/wrote	toys
family	sing	party/parties
friends	Christmas carols	each other
cards	hospital	

II. YES or NO?

1. December 22 is Christmas. _____

2. People decorate their houses. _____

3. It is a time to remember poor people. _____

4. Children write letters to Christopher Columbus. _____

5. People sing Christmas carols. _____

6. On Christmas Eve, many people go to school. _____

7. Children hang up their shoes. _____

III. MATCH:

1. Christmas tree _____

2. stocking _____

3. gift _____

4. Christmas card _____

5. Santa Claus _____

A.   B. Merry Christmas

C.   D.   E.

HOLIDAY SYMBOLS

Use these pictures for coloring, tracing, or making room and window decorations.

star	bell	candle
Santa Claus	sleigh	stocking
Christmas tree	present	candy cane
reindeer	dreidel	menorah

THE STORY OF CHRISTMAS

1. Two thousand years ago, the emperor Augustus wanted to count the people in his land. He told everyone to go back to the city where they had been born.

2. Joseph and Mary lived in Nazareth. Mary was going to have a baby. But they had to go to Bethlehem because Joseph had been born there. It was a long, long trip.

3. When they got to Bethlehem, the time came for the baby to be born. But there was no room for them to stay at the inn.

4. Joseph and Mary went to the stable. Mary's baby was born. They named him Jesus. Mary made a bed for the baby in a manger.

5. There were shepherds out in the fields. They were watching their sheep.

6. An angel came to speak to the shepherds. The shepherds were afraid.

7. "Don't be afraid," said the angel. "I bring you good news. Today, in the town of Bethlehem, a baby has been born. This baby is Christ the Lord. You will find him in a manger."

8. The shepherds went to Bethlehem. They found Mary and Joseph in the stable. They saw the baby in the manger. They were very happy.

9. A bright star appeared in the sky. Wise men saw the star in the East. "A new king is born," they said. "Let's go to see him. Let's bring him gifts."

THE STORY OF CHRISTMAS (continued)

10. The wise men followed the star. The star went ahead of them. It stopped over the place where the baby Jesus was born.

11. The wise men saw the child with his mother. They bowed down. "We have come to see the newborn king," they said.

12. They gave him gifts. They gave him gold. They gave him frankincense and myrrh. This was the first Christmas.

13. Today people give each other gifts on Christmas. They remember the gifts that the wise men gave to the baby Jesus.

THE STORY OF CHRISTMAS: EXERCISES

I. Do you know these words? Find these words in the story. Draw a line under them. Copy the words. Write the meanings.

thousand	manger	bring/brought
emperor	shepherd	follow/followed
count	sheep	Jesus
land	field	ahead
tell/told	angel	stop
city	be afraid	place
be born/was/were born	Lord	bow down/bowed down
trip	bright	newborn
room	star	gold
stay	wise men	frankincense
inn	East	myrrh
stable	king	

frankincense: incense; something that makes a very good smell when it burns

myrrh: incense or perfume

II. Complete the sentences.

1. Joseph and Mary lived in _____.

2. It was a _____ (long, short) way to Bethlehem.

3. There was no room at the _____.

4. _____ was born in the stable.

5. Shepherds were watching their _____.

6. An _____ spoke to the shepherds.

7. "Don't _____ _____. I bring you good news."

8. A bright _____ appeared in the sky.

9. The _____ followed the star.

10. The wise men gave _____ to the new born king.

WE WISH YOU A MERRY CHRISTMAS

We wish you a merry Christmas,
We wish you a merry Christmas,
We wish you a merry Christmas
And a Happy New Year.

JINGLE BELLS

Jingle bells, jingle bells,
Jingle all the way,
O what fun it is to ride
In a one-horse open sleigh, O

Jingle bells, jingle bells,
Jingle all the way,
O what fun it is to ride
In a one-horse open sleigh.

Dashing through the snow
In a one-horse open sleigh
O'er the fields we go
Laughing all the way.

Bells on bobtail ring,
Making spirits bright.
What fun it is to ride and sing
A sleighing song tonight.

Jingle bells, jingle bells,
Jingle all the way,
Oh what fun it is to ride
In a one-horse open sleigh, O

Jingle bells, jingle bells,
Jingle all the way,
Oh what fun it is to ride
In a one-horse open sleigh.

SILENT NIGHT

Silent night,   silent
Holy night,   holy
All is calm.   calm
All is bright.   bright
Round yon Virgin,   virgin
Mother and child,
Holy Infant, so tender and mild.   infant   tender   mild
Sleep in heavenly peace.   heavenly
Sleep in heavenly peace.   peace

Silent night,
Holy night.
Shepherds quake   shepherd   quake
At the sight.   sight
Glory streams from Heaven afar   glory   stream   afar
Heavenly hosts sing Hallelujah;   host
Christ the Savior is born,   savior
Christ the Savior is born.   be born

TEACHER'S CHOICE:
ACTIVITIES FOR WINTER HOLIDAYS

1. Have students make signs or posters with holiday greetings in their own language.

2. Make greeting cards. They can be as simple as line drawings with greetings on a folded page, or as elaborate as cutting and pasting projects using construction paper, foil, last year's cards, adding bits of cotton, felt, material, glitter, and any other materials you and your students choose. Encourage creativity!

   If you have a very small class, students can make line drawing greeting cards which you can duplicate so they have many copies of their art work to give or send as cards. (With a large class, students can be responsible for having their own cards reproduced outside of school, if they wish.) Students can make each card special by coloring and decorating them differently.

3. Make a holiday collage to decorate a bulletin board. Cut out pictures from magazines and old greeting cards. Use holiday gift wrap as a frame.

4. Enlarge the holiday symbols on page 97 for students to trace on colored paper. Hang in the window, from the ceiling, and so on.

5. Decorate a classroom tree. Students can each bring one ornament for the tree; or, make ornaments in class.

   a. Make, eat, and string popcorn.
   b. Cut strips of colored construction paper. Tape or glue them to make paper chains. You can also cut colorful strips from magazines to make paper chains.
   c. Wrap walnuts or small nuts with aluminum foil. First tape red or green curling ribbon to the walnuts to use for hanging them as ornaments.

6. Write a letter to Santa Claus from the class to tell what they want for the world for Christmas.

7. Make gifts for parents.

8. Have a grab bag gift exchange.

   > Write your name on a small piece of paper.
   > Put the paper in the bag.
   > Shake the bag. Mix up the names.
   > Take a paper from the bag and read the name.
   > Buy a present for the person whose name is on the paper you got.
   > Spend _____.

   Some gift suggestions: [Elicit and help with gift suggestions in the price range selected by the class.]

9. Play Winter Bingo, Hanukkah Bingo, or Christmas Bingo using words drawn from the reading lessons and activities.

10. Read "A Visit from St. Nicholas" from a well-illustrated book, pointing out vocabulary items as they are mentioned in the poem, using gestures and actions to make meanings clear.

SEASON'S GREETINGS AROUND THE WORLD

English: Merry Christmas

German: Froehliche Weihnachten

Spanish: Feliz Navidad

French: Joyeux Noël

Italian: Buon Natale

Portuguese: Boas Festas

Swedish: Glaedelig Jul

Dutch: Hartelijke Kerstgroeten

Hungarian: Boldog Karácsonyi Ünnepeket

Slovak: Vesele Vianoce

Hawaiian: Meli Kalikimaka

Eskimo: Quvianaqtuaq Kraisimagvik

Swahili: Salaam Kwa Siku Kuu

Russian: с рождеством (Srohzh dyést vom)

Greek: Καλά Χριστούγεννα (Kalla Christoughenna)

Japanese: メリークリスマス (Me ri Ku ree su ma su)

Korean: 메리 크리스마스 (Son tan ul chuka hamnidah)

Chinese: 聖誕快樂 (Sheng Tan Kuai Loh)

New Year's Eve is December 31. It is a noisy and happy time. People blow horns and ring bells on New Year's Eve.

Name _____ Date _____

THE NEW YEAR

1. When does a new year begin?

2. The calendar that we use is the Gregorian calendar. Our new year begins January first.

3. In ancient Egypt, the new year began when the Nile River flooded over its banks. In northern Europe, the new year began when the leaves fell off the trees.

4. In other parts of Europe, the new year began on the shortest day of the year (the winter solstice). In ancient Rome the new year was the first day of spring. This was the day when night and day were equal.

5. The Jewish New Year begins in September, at harvest time. The Chinese New Year begins in January or February.

6. A long time ago, many people thought that the spirits of dead people could come back on the last night of the year. People made loud noises on New Year's Eve to scare away bad spirits. They beat drums, rang bells, and exploded firecrackers or guns. In ancient Rome there was a whole week of wild behavior and drinking before the new year.

7. New Year's Eve is a holiday filled with fun. People are not afraid of spirits of dead people, but they still make a lot of noise!

THE NEW YEAR: EXERCISES

I. Do you know these words? Find these words in the story. Draw a line under them. Copy the words. Write the meanings.

begin/began	fall/fell	noises
calendar	winter solstice	scare
ancient	Rome	beat drums
Egypt	equal	explode/exploded
river	harvest	firecrackers
flood	think/thought	guns
bank	spirits	wild
northern	dead	behavior
Europe	loud	

II. 1. When is New Year's Day in your country?

_____

2. How do people celebrate New Year's Eve?

_____

3. How do they celebrate New Year's Day?

_____

4. Does your family do something special on New Year's Eve or New Year's Day? _____

Do you eat special foods? _____

Do you make resolutions? _____

NEW YEAR'S DAY

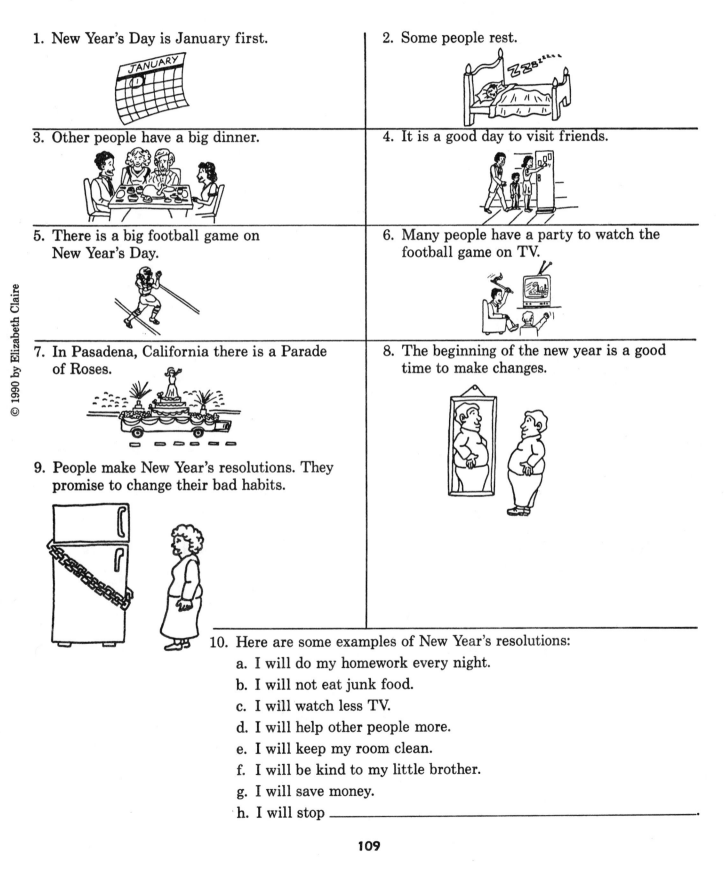

1. New Year's Day is January first.

2. Some people rest.

3. Other people have a big dinner.

4. It is a good day to visit friends.

5. There is a big football game on New Year's Day.

6. Many people have a party to watch the football game on TV.

7. In Pasadena, California there is a Parade of Roses.

8. The beginning of the new year is a good time to make changes.

9. People make New Year's resolutions. They promise to change their bad habits.

10. Here are some examples of New Year's resolutions:
    a. I will do my homework every night.
    b. I will not eat junk food.
    c. I will watch less TV.
    d. I will help other people more.
    e. I will keep my room clean.
    f. I will be kind to my little brother.
    g. I will save money.
    h. I will stop _____.

NEW YEAR'S DAY: EXERCISES

I. Do you know these words? Find these words in the story. Draw a line under them. Copy the words. Write the meanings.

new	rose	homework
year	beginning	less
January	time	junk food
rest	make/made changes	help
visit	resolutions	room
friend	promise	clean
football	change	save
game	bad habit	money
parade	example	stop

II. Discussion:

1. How will you (How did you) spend New Year's Day?

   _____

2. How do people spend New Year's Day in your country?

   _____

   _____

   _____

3. Is it a good idea to make New Year's resolutions? _____

4. It is easy to make resolutions, but it is not always easy to keep them. How can a person be sure to keep a resolution?

   _____

   _____

5. What resolutions will you make?

   _____

   _____

   _____

   _____

AFRICAN-AMERICAN HISTORY MONTH

1. The history of slavery is a very sad story.

2. Beginning in 1619, the first slaves came to America from Africa. In the South, there were big tobacco and cotton plantations. The plantation owners bought slaves to work for them.

3. Slaves picked cotton in the fields. They worked in the houses. They could not leave the plantations. They did not get paid for their work. Some slave owners were very cruel.

4. There were laws against slavery in the North. Many slaves ran away to the North.

5. From 1861–1865 there was a Civil War between the North and the South. After the Civil War, all slaves became free.

6. After the war there were still many problems for African-American people. They had no education. They could not vote. They earned very little money.

7. For many, many years, black people and white people were segregated (kept separate) by law. There were segregated schools, segregated movie houses, and segregated train cars.

8. Black people and white people could not go to the same restaurants, hotels, or swimming pools. They could not drink water from the same fountains or use the same bathrooms.

AFRICAN-AMERICAN HISTORY MONTH *(continued)*

9. Black people could not get good jobs. They could not find good places to live. They could not play in sports with white people.

10. When black people tried to change things, they were arrested and put into jail. They lost their jobs. Terrorists burned down their houses or killed people who "stepped out of line."

11. Some white people tried to help. It was dangerous. They could go to jail too. Terrorists burned their houses or killed them.

12. But still, there were many black and white leaders who worked all their lives to change some of these conditions.

13. Here are a few of these famous African-Americans:

14. **Harriet Tubman** was a slave, but she ran away to the North. Then she came back and showed other slaves the way to escape. She found white people who would help the runaways and hide them in the daytime.

15. **Frederick Douglass** was born a slave, but he ran away to the North. He made many speeches to tell people how bad slavery was. People cried when they heard him speak. They wanted to end slavery.

16. **Booker T. Washington** was born a slave but became free after the Civil War. He loved to learn, and he taught himself. He went to college and became a teacher. He started a college for black students, Tuskeegee Institute.

17. **W.E.B. DuBois** went to Harvard University. He wrote many books. He organized the National Association for the Advancement of Colored People (NAACP).

18. **Paul Robeson** was an athlete, an actor, a singer, and a lawyer. He made many speeches and sang songs about equality and justice. He moved to England where he felt more free.

19. **Malcolm Little**'s family was poor and had many problems. He became a robber and went to jail. In jail, he read books and became a Muslim. He changed his name to Malcolm X. When he got out of jail, he became a famous speaker. He told Americans how terrible it was to be black in America. He told African-Americans to fight for their rights.

20. **Martin Luther King, Jr.** was a minister of a church. He made speeches and led marches to change laws. He won a Nobel Peace Prize for his work.

21. **Jesse Jackson** was born very poor, with no father. He worked with Martin Luther King, and became a very good speaker. He ran for president in 1984 and 1988. He has done many good things for black and white people.

22. **Shirley Chisolm** was a Congresswoman from Brooklyn. She spoke for women's rights and black people's rights. She became a candidate for Vice President of the United States.

Name _____ Date _____

AFRICAN-AMERICAN HISTORY MONTH: EXERCISES

I. Do you know these words? Find these words in the story. Draw a line under them. Copy the words. Write the meanings.

history	vote	leaders
slaves	earn/earned	conditions
slavery	segregated	famous
Africa/African	separate	escape
tobacco	restaurants	runaways
cotton	hotels	hide
plantation	swimming pools	speech/speeches
owners	fountains	free
buy/bought	same	institute
pick	sports	university
fields	arrest/arrested	organize/organized
cruel	terrorists	association
law	burn/burned	advancement
Civil War	step/stepped out of line	athlete
problems	dangerous	lawyer
education	jail	equality
	justice	

II. Discuss. Then write the answers to the questions on a separate sheet of paper.
   1. What work did African slaves do in the South?
   2. Why did slaves run away to the North?
   3. What happened in 1861–1865?
   4. What problems did African-Americans have after they became free?
   5. How were black people and white people segregated?
   6. What happened to people who tried to change things?
   7. Who are some famous people who tried to change things?

III. Match:

   1. She showed slaves the way to escape to the North. _____   A. Jesse Jackson

   2. He made speeches in the North to tell people about   B. Harriet Tubman

      slavery. _____   C. Frederick Douglass

   3. He ran for president in 1984 and 1988. _____   D. Malcolm X

   4. He won a Nobel Peace Prize for his work. _____   E. Martin Luther King, Jr.

   5. He told black people to fight for their rights. _____   F. Paul Robeson

   6. He sang songs about equality and justice. _____

MARTIN LUTHER KING, JR.

January 15 is Martin Luther King, Jr.'s Birthday. Martin Luther King, Jr. was a great American. He worked hard for black people and poor people. He was a great speaker. He won the Nobel Peace Prize.

THE MONTGOMERY BUS BOYCOTT

1. One day Rosa Parks got on a bus. She was very tired. She sat down.

2. HEY! YOU CAN'T SIT DOWN. GIVE YOUR SEAT TO A WHITE PERSON.

3. I'M TOO TIRED. I'LL SIT RIGHT HERE.

4. YOU CAN'T. I'LL STOP THE BUS AND CALL THE POLICE!

5. The police came. They arrested Rosa.

6. Black people were angry. WHAT CAN WE DO?

THE MONTGOMERY BUS BOYCOTT (continued)

7.

DON'T RIDE THEIR BUSES. WE CAN WALK TO WORK.

8.

GOOD IDEA! THE BUS COMPANY NEEDS OUR MONEY. THEY WILL HAVE TO CHANGE THE LAWS IF THEY WANT US TO RIDE THEIR BUSES.

9. So black people stopped riding the buses. They walked to work.

10. "That's not fair!" said the bus owners. The police arrested Martin Luther King and put him in jail.

11. The black people would not ride the buses.

12. After one year, the law changed. Black and white people could sit in any seat on the bus. It was a great day for all people.

THE MONTGOMERY BUS BOYCOTT: EXERCISES

I. Do you know these words? Find these words in the story. Draw a line under them. Copy the words. Write the meanings.

bus	arrest	walk
tired	angry	work
black	good idea	fair
white	bus company	owners
person	change	jail
right here	law	lose/lost
police	stop	seat
call	ride/rode	

II. Choose the best answer:

1. Rosa Parks was _____. (black, white)

2. She sat in the _____ of the bus.   (front, back)

3. The bus driver called _____.   (Martin Luther King, the police)

4. Martin Luther King said, "We can _____ to work."   (ride the bus, walk)

5. The police put Martin Luther King _____.   (in jail, in the front of the bus)

6. The bus companies lost a lot of _____.   (buses, money)

7. After one _____ the law changed and now people can sit in any seat on a bus.   (month, year)

THE STORY OF MARTIN LUTHER KING, JR.

1. Martin Luther King, Jr. was born in Atlanta, Georgia on January 15, 1929. He became a minister like his father, Martin Luther King, Sr.

2. Many laws in southern states were not fair to African-Americans. They could not vote, so they could not change the laws.

3. It was not possible for one person alone to change this.

4. Martin Luther King, Jr. was a powerful speaker. People listened to him. "Many people working together can change things," he said.

5. "Use love, not violence," he said. He made speeches. He wrote books. He helped black people to register to vote.

6. He was arrested and put into jail. When he got out of jail, he continued to make speeches.

7. It was dangerous work. His house was bombed. Schools and churches were bombed too.

THE STORY OF MARTIN LUTHER KING, JR. (continued)

8. In 1964, Martin Luther King, Jr. received one of the world's greatest honors, the Nobel Peace Prize.

9. He worked for all poor people, white and black, Indian and Mexican. He spoke against the war in Vietnam.

10. On April 4, 1968, King was in Memphis, Tennessee to lead a march for poor workers. An assassin shot him and he died.

11. Martin Luther King, Jr. was a great American. His most famous speech was at the March on Washington, August 28, 1963.

12. ". . . I have a dream. I have a dream that one day this nation will . . . live out the true meaning of its creed, 'We hold these truths to be self-evident: that all men are created equal'

13. ". . . . I have a dream that my four little children will one day live in a nation where they will not be judged by the color of their skin but by the content of their character."

14. Many laws have changed since 1963, but Martin Luther King's dream is still a dream. There is a lot of work for all of us to do.

THE STORY OF MARTIN LUTHER KING, JR.: EXERCISES

I. Do you know these words? Find these words in the story. Draw a line under them. Copy the words. Write the meanings.

Jr. = junior	violence	famous
be born; is/was born	register to vote	dream
minister	arrest	nation
Sr. = senior	jail	meaning
law	continue	creed
southern	dangerous	true/truth
fair	bomb	self-evident
change	receive	equal
vote	honor	create
possible	Nobel Peace Prize	judge
alone	war in Vietnam	skin
powerful	lead/led	content
speaker	assassin	character
work together	shoot/shot	

II. Choose the best answer:

1. Martin Luther King, Jr. was a ———————————————— like his father.   (minister, lawyer)

2. Black people could not ———————————————— so they could not change the laws. (work, vote)

3. "Use ————————————————, not violence," said Martin Luther King, Jr. (guns, love)

4. It was dangerous work. His ———————————————— was bombed.   (house, book)

5. Martin Luther King, Jr. received the Nobel ———————————————— Prize. (Peace, speech)

6. In 1968, an assassin ———————————————— Martin Luther King, Jr.   (arrested, killed)

7. Martin Luther King, Jr. had a dream that all people would be treated as ————————————. (equals, children)

INAUGURATION DAY

1. Every four years, Americans elect a new president. The election is in November. The new president begins to work on January 20. This day is called Inauguration Day. *Inauguration* means beginning.

2. There is a big parade in Washington, D.C. Soldiers, bands, and beautiful floats parade down Pennsylvania Avenue. Thousands of people come to see the parade.

3. Other people watch the inauguration on television. All the "VIPs" in the government are there. (VIP = very important person)

4. The Chief Justice of the Supreme Court inaugurates the President. The new president puts his or her hand on the Bible and declares:

5. "I do solemnly swear that I will faithfully execute the office of the President of the United States and will to the best of my ability preserve, protect, and defend the Constitution of the United States."

6. Then the new president makes a speech. The new president tells the American people what he or she plans to do.

7. In the evening, there are many parties, or balls. People celebrate the inauguration. The President goes to many of these inaugural balls. The President greets the VIPs and the people who helped with the election.

INAUGURATION DAY: VOCABULARY BUILDING

I. Do you know these words? Find these words in the story. Draw a line under them. Copy the words. Write the meanings.

inaugurate	solemnly
inauguration	swear
elect	faithfully
election	execute
president	ability
beginning	preserve
parade	protect
soldiers	defend
band	constitution
ceremony	speech
VIP	plan
chief justice	celebrate
Supreme Court	inaugural ball
Bible	greet
declare	

II. Answer:

1. What happens on Inauguration Day? _____

2. When is Inauguration Day? _____

3. Who is the new president of the United States?

_____

4. Who is the new vice president?

_____

5. Who are some other VIPs?

_____

_____

_____

6. What does the new president declare when he is inaugurated?

_____

_____

7. What happens in the evening? _____

CHINESE NEW YEAR

Chinese New Year is _____. This is the year _____, the year of the _____.

ALL ABOUT CHINESE NEW YEAR

1. Chinese New Year is _____.

2. This is the year of the _____.

3. Many Chinese people live in the big cities of the United States. In "Chinatown" there is a parade with a large "dragon" and people in costumes. The dragon leads the people into a good new year.

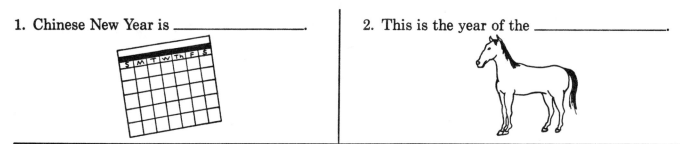

4. Many visitors go to see the parades. There are loud noises and firecrackers. The air is full of smoke and the smell of gunpowder.

5. People say "Gong Hay Fat Choy." That means "Have a Happy New Year."

6. The New Year is a giant birthday party. Everyone is one year older on this day. They exchange presents and play games.

7. Parents give children money. The money is in red envelopes for good luck.

8. The Chinese make delicious foods for the New Year. They put flowers in their homes. They visit their family and friends.

9. Koreans, Japanese, and some other Asians celebrate the New Year on this date.

CHINESE NEW YEAR: EXERCISES

I. Do you know these words? Find these words in the story. Draw a line under them. Copy the words. Write the meanings.

Chinese	loud	giant
Chinatown	noises	exchange
parade	firecrackers	presents
dragon	air	money
costumes	full	envelopes
lead/led	smoke	good luck
visitors	smell	delicious
birthday	gunpowder	celebrate

II. Complete the sentences and answer the questions.

1. This is the year of the _____.

2. A _____ leads the parade in Chinatown.

3. People say _____. That means "Happy New Year."

4. All Chinese celebrate their _____ on the New Year.

5. Parents give children _____ in _____ envelopes for good luck.

III. Activities for Chinese New Year:

1. Learn the names of Asian countries and locate them on a world map.

2. Make paper dragons.

3. Read an Asian folktale.

4. Have an Asian foods tasting party.

5. Videotape the news broadcast of the New Year celebration and view it in class.

THE YEAR OF THE . . .

What animal rules the year in which you were born?

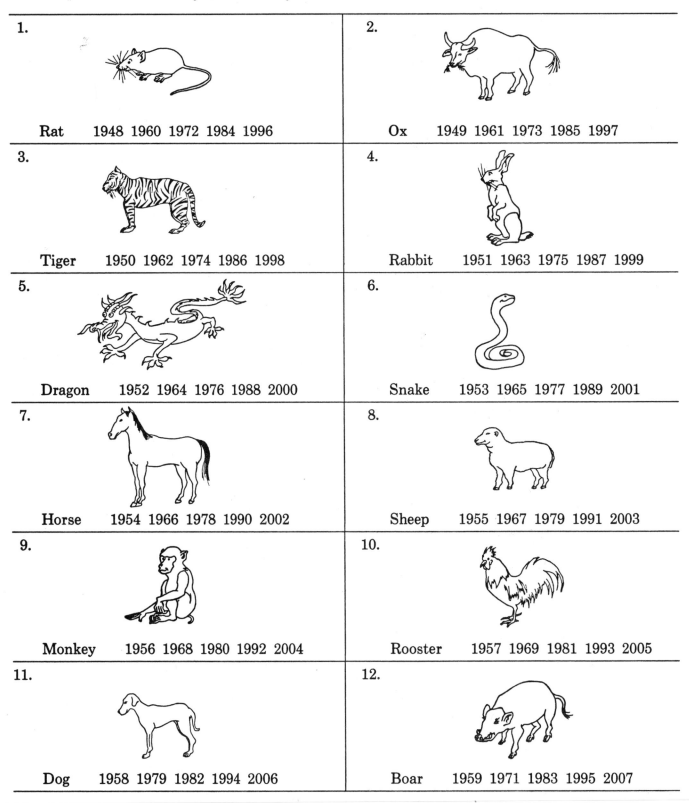

1.

Rat   1948 1960 1972 1984 1996

2.

Ox   1949 1961 1973 1985 1997

3.

Tiger   1950 1962 1974 1986 1998

4.

Rabbit   1951 1963 1975 1987 1999

5.

Dragon   1952 1964 1976 1988 2000

6.

Snake   1953 1965 1977 1989 2001

7.

Horse   1954 1966 1978 1990 2002

8.

Sheep   1955 1967 1979 1991 2003

9.

Monkey   1956 1968 1980 1992 2004

10.

Rooster   1957 1969 1981 1993 2005

11.

Dog   1958 1979 1982 1994 2006

12.

Boar   1959 1971 1983 1995 2007

ABRAHAM LINCOLN'S BIRTHDAY

ABRAHAM LINCOLN

Abraham Lincoln's birthday is February 12. Lincoln was the sixteenth president of the United States. He was a very wise and kind leader.

THE LIFE OF ABRAHAM LINCOLN

1. Abraham Lincoln was born in Kentucky on February 12, 1809. His family was very poor.

2. Abe loved to learn. He walked many miles to school every day.

3. At night he did his homework by the light of the fireplace.

4. He became a lawyer. He lived in Illinois. People called him "Honest Abe."

5. One day, he visited the South. He saw people buying slaves. Abe said, "It is wrong for people to have slaves. Some day all people shall be free." He wanted to become president of the United States.

6. Many people in the North said, "Lincoln is right. The slaves should be free."

7. People in the South said, "Lincoln is wrong. Each state can make its own laws about slaves. We need slaves to grow cotton and tobacco."

8. In 1860, Abraham Lincoln won the election. He became the sixteenth president of the United States.

Name _____ Date _____

THE LIFE OF ABRAHAM LINCOLN *(continued)*

9. Eleven states did not want to be part of the United States. They formed a new country. They called their country "The Confederate States of America."

10. But Lincoln said, "The states must stay united." A terrible war began between the North and the South. It was called the Civil War. Many people died in this war.

11. At last, in 1865, the Civil War ended. The South lost and came back into the union. The slaves were free. Lincoln had saved the country.

12. Black people were very happy to be free. The people of the North were happy too. Lincoln planned ways to help the South after the war. He wanted the whole country to work together again.

13. But the people in the South were not happy. Many of them hated Lincoln. John Wilkes Booth was from the South. He was a famous actor. He planned to kill Lincoln.

14. On April 14, 1865, Lincoln went to the theater. John Wilkes Booth had a gun. He shot and killed Lincoln.

15. Many people cried for many, many days after Lincoln died. He was the greatest leader they had ever known.

THE LIFE OF ABRAHAM LINCOLN: EXERCISES

I. Do you know these words? Find these words in the story. Draw a line under them. Copy the words. Write the meanings.

be born/was born	state	Civil War
family	laws	lose/lost
poor	grow/grew	save/saved
mile	cotton	plan/planned
fireplace	tobacco	work together
lawyer	election	hate/hated
visit/visited	country	actor
buy/bought	confederate	kill
slaves	united	theater
wrong	terrible	gun
free	war	shoot/shot
president	between	great/greatest
	leader	

II. Complete the sentences.

1. Abraham Lincoln ———————————— in Kentucky, on February 12, 1809.

2. Lincoln became a ————————————.

3. When Lincoln saw people buying slaves he said, "It is ———————————— for people to have slaves."

4. In 1860, he became the sixteenth ———————————— of the United States.

5. Eleven southern states formed a new ————————————.

6. They called their country the ———————————— States of America.

7. Many people died in the ———————————— War between the North and the South.

8. After the war, the ———————————— were free.

9. ———————————— shot and killed Abraham Lincoln.

10. Americans will always remember Abraham Lincoln because:

————————————————————————————————————

————————————————————————————————————

————————————————————————————————————

THE LIFE OF ABRAHAM LINCOLN: EXERCISES (continued)

III. Match:

1. slave _____

2. Civil War _____

3. Confederate States of America _____

4. Abraham Lincoln _____

5. John Wilkes Booth _____

A. Sixteenth President of the United States

B. A famous actor who killed Lincoln

C. The war between the North and the South

D. A person who is not free and works without pay

E. A new country formed by eleven southern states that did not want to be united with the northern states

IV. Activities:

1. Discover the ways Americans remember and honor Abraham Lincoln. Ask American students. See if you can count ten different ways.

2. Watch a filmstrip or video about the life of Abraham Lincoln.

VALENTINE'S DAY

Name _____   Date _____

ALL ABOUT SAINT VALENTINE'S DAY

1. Valentine's Day is February 14.

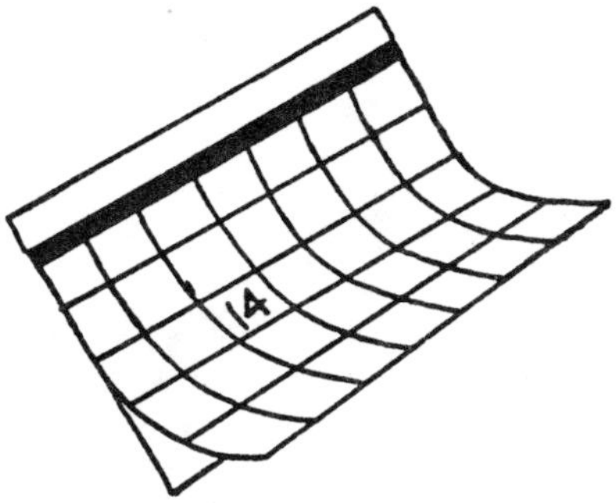

2. It is a day for love and friendship.

3. We can give Valentine cards to people we love.

4. Cards can have hearts, flowers, lace, and pretty poems on them.

5. One very old poem is this:

Roses are red,

Violets are blue;

Sugar is sweet,

And so are you.

Do you know these words?

Valentine	flower	violet
love	lace	sugar
friendship	poem	sweet
card	rose	So are you
heart		

February 14 is Valentine's Day.

Name _____   Date _____

THE STORY OF CUPID

This is one story people think about on Valentine's Day:

1. Cupid is the god of love. He is a small baby with magic arrows.

2. Cupid likes to make people fall in love. But he is only a baby, so he is not very smart.

3. Cupid shoots his magic arrows into someone's heart.

4. Then that person falls in love with the next person he or she sees.

5. Cupid does not always shoot a magic arrow into the other person's heart. Then the other person does not love the first person.

6. Cupid makes a lot of trouble this way.

YUK!

I. Do you know these words? Find these words in the story. Draw a line under them. Copy the words. Write the meanings.

god   only a baby
magic   shoot
arrow   person
fall/fell in love   trouble
smart

II. Discuss:

1. Who is Cupid?
2. Is he very smart? Why not?
3. What happens when Cupid shoots his magic arrow into someone's heart?
4. How does Cupid make a lot of trouble?

HOW DID SAINT VALENTINE'S DAY BEGIN?

1. There are many different stories about the origin of Saint Valentine's Day.

2. Valentine was a priest in Rome a long time ago. He was a very good priest and many people liked him.

3. Claudius, the Roman emperor, did not want young men to get married. Claudius wanted men to go to war. He said no one could get married without his permission.

4. Young couples wanted to get married. Valentine married them in secret. When Claudius found out, he put Valentine into prison. Claudius killed Valentine on February 14.

5. Two hundred years later, the church made February 14 a special day to remember Saint Valentine. Valentine became the patron saint of lovers.

6. A different story is that February 14 is the day that birds choose their mates, so people also choose the ones they will love on that day.

I. Do you know these words? Find them in the story. Draw a line under them. Copy the words. Write the meanings.

origin	war	the church
priest	couple	patron saint
Rome	in secret	lover
emperor	find out/found out	choose/chose
married	prison	mate

II. Discuss:

1. Do you celebrate Valentine's Day in your country?

2. What are the customs?

3. What other customs are there for young couples who are in love?

4. Are there special ways for young men and young women to meet each other?

SUSAN B. ANTHONY DAY

SUSAN B. ANTHONY

Susan B. Anthony was a great American. She worked for the rights of women.

THE STORY OF SUSAN B. ANTHONY

1. February 15 is Susan B. Anthony Day.

2. Susan B. Anthony was born on February 15, 1820. She learned to read and write when she was three years old. She became a teacher.

3. She worked hard to end slavery for black people. She went to many meetings. One day she stood up at the meeting to speak.

4. "Women may not speak at our meetings," said the leader. "Women may only listen."

5. "We can do much more if we can speak. Women have something to say, too," said Susan.

6. After the Civil War, the slaves were free. Susan B. Anthony saw that women were still not free. Black and white men could vote, but what about women?

7. On Election Day, Susan went with fifteen women and voted. She was arrested. The judge said she must pay $100 because she broke the law.

8. "This law is not fair," she said. She would not pay.

9. Susan B. Anthony made many speeches. People threw rotten eggs and rotten tomatoes at her. She wrote a newspaper. She joined with other women who wanted women's rights.

10. She worked for women's rights for forty years. Four states gave women the right to vote by 1906, when she died. In 1920, the Nineteenth Amendment was added to the Constitution. It gives women the right to vote. It is sometimes called "The Susan B. Anthony Amendment."

11. In February, we remember Susan B. Anthony and other women who changed the way people think about men and women. Today girls can have the same education as boys. They can choose almost any career. Men can choose more careers, too.

SUSAN B. ANTHONY DAY: EXERCISES

I. Do you know these words? Find these words in the story. Draw a line under them. Copy the words. Write the meanings.

slavery	arrested	join/joined
meeting	break/broke the law	women's rights
stand/stood	fair	Constitution
Civil War	speech/speeches	amendment
free	rotten	education
vote	eggs	choose/chose
		career

II. Complete the sentences:

1. Susan B. Anthony was born _____, 1820.

2. Susan B. Anthony worked hard to end _____ for black people.

3. After the Civil War, Anthony saw that women were still not _____.

4. When she tried to vote, she was _____.

5. She worked for women's rights for _____ years.

6. The Nineteenth Amendment to the Constitution gives women the right to _____.

III. Discuss:

1. Can women vote in your country?

2. In your country do men and women have different jobs in the family?

3. What work is for men only?

4. What work is for women only?

5. Do boys and girls go to the same schools?

6. Do you think boys and girls should be treated equally?

7. Find out: What new jobs can women do today that only men could do before? What jobs can men do that only women did before?

8. Find out: In what ways are men and women, or boys and girls, still not treated equally? Do you think this should change?

GEORGE WASHINGTON'S BIRTHDAY

GEORGE WASHINGTON

George Washington was the first president of the United States. He is called "the Father of His Country." His birthday is February 22.

THE STORY OF GEORGE WASHINGTON

1. George Washington was born February 22, 1732 in Virginia. His family was rich. They owned a large plantation. George loved parties and dancing.

2. He was very kind. He gave money to many poor people.

3. George Washington is called "the Father of His Country." He was the leader of the American army in the War of Independence. He did not ask for any pay for this.

4. The war was very difficult. One winter at Valley Forge the soldiers had no warm clothes or shoes. But they did not leave George Washington. He was a good leader and they loved him.

5. The Americans won the war. A new country, the United States, was born. After the war George Washington was the leader of the men who wrote the Constitution for the new country.

6. George Washington was tired. He did not want to be president. But everyone voted for him. He was elected the first president of the United States.

7. He was a very good president. He was elected a second time in 1793. He was "first in war, first in peace, and first in the hearts of his countrymen."

THE STORY OF GEORGE WASHINGTON: EXERCISES

I. Do you know these words? Find them in the story. Draw a line under them. Copy the words. Write the meanings.

be/was born	country	soldier
rich	leader	clothes
own	army	win/won
plantation	war	constitution
party	independence	tired
kind	difficult	elect
president	father	peace
	countrymen	

II. Complete the sentences:

1. George Washington was born ————————————— ————, ————.

2. George Washington is called the ————————————— of his country.

3. He was the leader in the American War for —————————————.

4. George Washington was the first ————————————— of the United States.

III. Write "Lincoln" or "Washington" after these sentences.

1. He was born in Kentucky. —————————————

2. He was born in Virginia. —————————————

3. He was the first president. —————————————

4. He was the sixteenth president. —————————————

5. He fought in the War of Independence. —————————————

6. He was president during the Civil War. —————————————

7. He freed the slaves. —————————————

8. He saved the Union. —————————————

9. He helped to write the Constitution. —————————————

10. He was a good leader. —————————————

GEORGE WASHINGTON AND THE CHERRY TREE

There are many stories about George Washington. Here is one famous story:

1. When George Washington was a little boy, his father gave him an ax for his birthday.

2. George wanted to practice with his ax, so he cut down a tree near his house.

3. When George's father came home, he saw that his favorite cherry tree had been cut down. He was very, very angry. "Who cut down my cherry tree?" he shouted.

4. George was very afraid. He was sure that his father would punish him. But he did not tell a lie.

5. "Father," said George, "I cannot tell a lie. I cut down your cherry tree with my new ax."

6. "My son," said George's father. "I am sad that I have lost my cherry tree. But you have given me something better. You told the truth. That makes me a very happy father." He hugged and kissed George and did not punish him.

7. Today, many people eat cherry pie on Washington's birthday and tell this story to children.

What happened first? Write the number 1. What happened next? Write the number 2, then 3, 4, and 5 to show what happened next.

_____ George cut down the cherry tree.

_____ George told the truth.

_____ George got an ax for his birthday.

_____ George's father was angry.

_____ George's father was happy.

GEORGE WASHINGTON AND THE CHERRY TREE: EXERCISES

I. Do you know these words? Find these words in the story. Draw a line under them. Copy the words. Write the meanings.

ax	favorite	punish
birthday	cherry	lie
practice	angry	tell a lie/told a lie
cut down	shout	tell the truth/told the truth
tree	afraid	hug/hugged
near	sure	kiss/kissed

II. Activities:

1. Make a comic strip showing the story of George Washington and the cherry tree. Use a large piece of drawing paper. Divide the paper into six parts. Draw pictures to show what happened. Write the words that George and his father say.

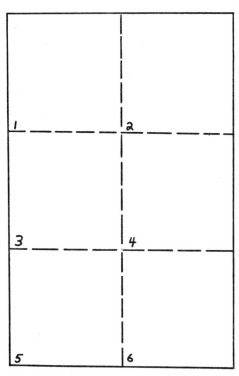

2. Talk about the ways Americans remember George Washington:
   - Look at George Washington's portrait on the quarter and dollar bill.
   - Washington, D.C., the state of Washington, schools, streets, and many other places and things are named for him.
   - The Washington Monument was built in his honor.
   - His home, Mount Vernon, is open to visitors.
3. Serve and eat cherry pie.

PRESIDENTS FIND-A-WORD

Can you find these words in the puzzle?

George Washington	president	leader	independence
war	father	slaves	birthday
Abraham Lincoln	south	civil	free
north	country	honest	

```
W  H  L  G  E  O  S  O  H  O  N  I  N  G
A  A  P  E  W  B  Y  S  O  U  T  H  S  L
S  N  R  O  A  I  S  L  N  L  A  V  L  I
L  E  P  R  E  S  I  D  E  N  T  P  A  R
M  L  T  G  T  R  A  V  S  R  E  S  V  T
T  R  S  E  H  N  O  R  T  H  I  D  E  B
R  O  R  W  D  A  E  S  N  O  R  S  S  I
A  B  R  A  H  A  M  L  I  N  C  O  L  N
M  I  N  S  A  B  R  E  N  T  O  C  E  R
E  R  O  H  A  H  A  M  E  F  U  I  A  L
L  T  R  I  L  I  N  E  R  E  N  V  D  I
I  H  S  N  C  O  R  L  N  E  T  B  E  V
T  D  O  G  C  F  A  T  H  E  R  I  R  I
Q  A  U  T  G  E  O  R  A  B  Y  R  A  C
R  Y  T  O  H  A  M  L  I  H  O  N  S  O
S  T  I  N  D  E  P  E  N  D  E  N  C  E
```

Name _____   Date _____

FEBRUARY 29

1. The earth takes 365 days and six hours to go around the sun.

2. Our calendar has 365 days. Every fourth year has an extra day. The year with 366 days is a *leap year*.

$4\overline{)1988}$

$4\overline{)1992}$

$4\overline{)1996}$

$4\overline{)2000}$

3. A year that can be divided by 4 is a leap year. 1988, 1992, and 1996 are leap years.

4. A year that ends in 00 is a leap year only if it can be divided by 400. The year 2000 is a leap year.

5. The extra day is added to the month of February. Children who are born on February 29 must celebrate their birthday on February 28 or March 1 in years that are not leap years.

I. Do you know these words? Find these words in the story. Draw a line under them. Copy the words. Write the meanings.

earth	calendar	divide/be divided by
takes (time)	fourth	that ends in 00
hours	extra	celebrate
go around	leap year	

II. Fill in the blanks and answer the question.

1. It takes the earth _____ days and _____ hours to go around the

_____ .

2. Will these years be leap years?

a. 2004   b. 2046   c. 2088   d. 3000   e. 4000

Name _____ Date _____

SAINT PATRICK'S DAY

Name ————————————————————— Date ————————

ALL ABOUT SAINT PATRICK'S DAY

1. St. Patrick's Day is March 17. Schools, banks, and post offices are not closed.

2. St. Patrick is the patron saint of Ireland. Many Irish people came to live in America. They brought their holiday with them.

3. People who are not Irish can enjoy St. Patrick's Day, too. There are parades on St. Patrick's Day. Bagpipes play Irish music. People dance jigs (a very fast dance) and sing Irish songs.

4. Green is everywhere on St. Patrick's Day. People wear green clothes: green shirts, green socks, green ties, or just a green flower or ribbon. Green coloring is added to cakes, cookies, and even beer.

5. Favorite foods on this day are corned beef and cabbage and Irish stew (lamb, onions, and potatoes cooked in a thick gravy).

6. Symbols of St. Patrick's Day are the shamrock (a three-leaf clover), the shillelagh (sha′lā lee; a wooden club) and leprechauns (lép re kahns; tiny little men).

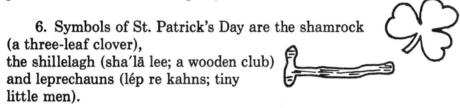

Name _____ Date _____

SAINT PATRICK'S DAY: EXERCISES

I. Do you know these words? Find these words in the story. Draw a line under them. Copy the words. Write the meanings.

saint	band	cabbage
patron saint	symbol	stew
Ireland	dance	jig
Irish	Irish jig	symbol
parade	clothes	shamrock
bagpipes	coloring	shillelagh
music	beer	leprechaun
green	corned beef	

II. Answer the questions:

1. What holiday is March 17th? _____

2. Are schools closed or open? _____

3. St. Patrick is the patron saint of _____. (Ireland, the United States)

4. People wear the color _____ on St. Patrick's Day.

5. What are some things people do on St. Patrick's Day?

_____

_____

_____

III. Match:

1. A three-leaf clover _____   A. an Irish jig

2. A wooden club _____   B. shamrock

3. Tiny little men _____   C. potatoes, onions and lamb

4. Irish stew _____   D. leprechauns

5. A very fast dance _____   E. shillelagh

LEPRECHAUNS

1. The Irish people tell stories about tiny people no bigger than your little finger. These little people are called *leprechauns*.

2. Leprechauns are very smart. They are full of tricks. They live in the woods, where they gather gold and bury it. It is very hard to see leprechauns because they run and hide when humans are around.

3. The Irish say that if you can catch a leprechaun, you can make him tell you where his gold is buried. Then you will be richer than all the kings on the earth. But watch out for tricks!

4. Jack was a boy who wanted to be rich. He was sure he could catch a leprechaun and find out where his gold was. Jack waited and watched, and watched and waited ever so quietly in the woods. Day after day, he watched and waited.

5. At last, one day he saw a tiny man with long white hair and a long white beard. He swooped his hand over the leprechaun and zap! The leprechaun was caught!

6. "Let me go, human!" shouted the leprechaun in a tiny voice. Jack held him safely inside his two hands. The leprechaun struggled and kicked furiously.

7. "First, tell me where your gold is buried," said Jack.

8. "Yes, yes. I will tell you," said the little man. "It is buried under a tree. Just walk where I tell you and I will show you."

9. So Jack walked deep into the woods with the leprechaun. They came to a place where the trees were very close together. The leprechaun pointed to a tree and said, "Here. My gold is buried under this tree."

LEPRECHAUNS (continued)

10. Now Jack knew that this was true, because leprechauns never tell lies. But it was a very plain tree. It looked the same as all the other trees around it.

11. "I will have to go home to get a shovel," said Jack, "but I don't want to forget which tree the gold is under."

12. He had a yellow scarf around his neck. He took the scarf off and tied it around the tree.

13. "You must promise me that you won't take my yellow scarf off this tree," Jack said to the leprechaun.

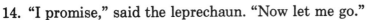

14. "I promise," said the leprechaun. "Now let me go."

15. Leprechauns are tricky, but Jack knew that they always keep their promises. So he knelt down to the ground. He opened his hand and let the little fellow go. The leprechaun ran off into the woods and was quickly out of sight.

16. Jack ran as fast as he could to get a shovel. He was very excited and happy.

17. He found a shovel and ran back with it into the woods. Soon he would be richer than any king on earth, he thought.

18. But when he got to the deep part of the woods where the trees were close together, what do you think he saw? Every tree had a yellow scarf tied around it, exactly like his own scarf. Hundreds and hundreds of trees. Thousands of trees. As far as he could see, every tree had a yellow scarf tied around it.

19. Jack's mouth hung open. Tears came to his eyes. Which tree was the gold buried under? There was no way that he could dig under all of those trees. So Jack very sadly went home. He was one more person who had been tricked by a leprechaun.

LEPRECHAUNS: EXERCISES

I. Do you know these words? Find these words in the story. Draw a line under them. Copy the words. Write the meanings.

Irish	wait	true
tiny	quiet/quietly	tell/told lies
leprechaun	day after day	plain
tricks	at last	look/looked the same
woods	beard	shovel
gold	swoop	forget/forgot
bury/buried	zap!	scarf
hide/hid	shout/shouted	tie/tied
human	safe/safely	tricky
catch/caught	struggle	keep/kept a promise
rich/richer	kick/kicked	kneel/knelt
king	furious/furiously	excited
earth	deep	close together
watch out	point/pointed	exactly like
find out/found out	hang/hung	

II. YES or NO?

1. Leprechauns are bigger than humans. _____

2. Leprechauns have a lot of gold. _____

3. It is easy to catch a leprechaun. _____

4. Leprechauns always tell lies. _____

5. Leprechauns always keep their promises. _____

6. Leprechauns are very tricky. _____

III. What happened first? Write number 1 next to the sentence. What happened next? Write number 2, then 3, 4, 5, and 6.

_____ 1. Jack ran to get a shovel.

_____ 2. Jack very sadly went home.

_____ 3. The leprechaun showed Jack where the gold was buried.

_____ 4. Jack tied a yellow scarf around the tree.

_____ 5. Jack caught a leprechaun.

_____ 6. Every tree had a yellow scarf tied around it.

THE LEGEND OF ST. PATRICK

1. Maewyn was a young Christian who lived in Scotland. When he was sixteen, he was captured by Irish pirates. The pirates sold him as a slave.

2. The Irish were not Christians. After six years working for an Irish master, Maewyn was able to run away and leave Ireland. He vowed he would come back to Ireland some day and teach the Christian religion to the Irish people.

3. Maewyn became a priest in the Christian church. Later he became a bishop. In the year 431, the Pope gave him the name Patricius (Patrick). The Pope sent him to Ireland. "Take Christianity to Ireland," said the Pope.

4. Patrick went into each town in Ireland. A man walked in front of him, beating on drums. The drums announced that Patrick was coming into the town.

5. Patrick was very brave. He faced many dangers. The Irish threw stones at him. They put him into prison. But he got out. And he never gave up.

6. He taught people about Jesus Christ. The people became Christians. He baptized them. He started schools and churches.

7. An important idea of Christianity is that there are three parts of God in one: the Father, the Son, and the Holy Spirit. The Irish people could not understand how three could be the same as one. So Patrick used the shamrock to help them understand. With the three leaves of the shamrock, he showed how the three parts made up the whole.

8. Patrick worked in Ireland for forty years. He died on March 17, 493. Many years later, the church made him a Saint.

9. There are many legends of miracles that St. Patrick did. He healed sick people. Some legends tell that he healed dead people too. One story tells that he made snow burn. Another story tells that St. Patrick chased all the snakes out of Ireland by beating on his drum. There are no snakes in Ireland today.

Name _____ Date _____

THE LEGEND OF ST. PATRICK: EXERCISES

I. Do you know these words? Find these words in the story. Draw a line under them. Copy the words. Write the meanings.

Scotland	bishop	Holy Spirit
capture	the Pope	shamrock
pirate	beat on a drum	leaf/leaves
sell/sold	announce	legend
slave	brave	miracle
master	danger	heal
vow	throw stones	snake
religion	prison	
priest	baptize	

II. Choose the best answer.

1. Maewyn was a _____. (young Christian boy, Irish pirate)

2. He was captured by _____. (Christians, pirates)

3. He vowed he would bring the Christian religion to _____.

   (the Pope, Ireland)

4. The Pope gave Maewyn the name _____. (Patrick, Jesus)

5. A man beat on a _____ as Patrick walked into each

   town.   (drum, snake)

6. He taught the Irish about _____. (Jesus Christ, pirates)

7. He used the _____ to explain that the three parts of God are

   one.   (shamrock, snow)

8. There are no _____ in Ireland today.   (people, snakes)

Name _____

Date _____

SPRING

How many signs of spring can you find in this picture?

THE FIRST DAY OF SPRING

The first day of spring is March 20 or 21. It is the day when the night is as long as the day. This is called the spring equinox.

Signs of spring:

1. Grass begins to grow in the spring. Leaves begin to grow on the trees.

2. Flowers begin to grow. Bugs come out, and birds fly back from the south.

3. Birds sing and build nests in the spring.

4. Bears and other sleeping animals wake up.

5. Farmers and gardeners plant seeds in the spring.

6. Many people clean their houses completely for spring.

7. Baseball season begins in the spring.

8. Other spring games are marbles, hopscotch, and rollerskating.

9. Late spring is a favorite time for weddings.

SPRING: EXERCISES

I. Do you know these words? Find these words in the story. Draw a line under them. Copy the words. Write the meanings.

spring	flowers	gardeners
first	bugs	plant
night	birds	seeds
day	fly/flew	clean
as long as	south	completely
sign	sing	baseball
grass	build/built a nest	season
grow/grew	bears	game
leaf/leaves	wake up	hopscotch
trees	farmers	weddings

II. Answer:

1. When is the first day of spring? _____

2. Flowers begin to _____ .

3. Birds fly back from the _____ .

4. Birds build _____ in the spring.

5. Sleeping animals _____ in the spring.

6. Farmers plant _____ in the spring.

7. _____ season begins in the spring.

8. Another spring game is _____ .

9. A favorite time for _____ is in the late spring.

III. EARLY SPRING ACTIVITIES:

1. Go on a neighborhood trip. Look for signs of spring.

2. Plant a variety of seeds in a classroom garden. Observe their growth. Measure the differences between different seedlings.

3. Learn rhymes and chants from children's outdoor spring games.

WHAT'S WRONG WITH THIS PICTURE?

Name _____ Date _____

APRIL FOOL'S DAY

1. The first day of April is full of fun. It is April Fool's Day.

2. A fool is a person who does not think carefully. A fool easily believes things that are not true.

3. On April Fool's Day, people tell lies to fool other people. They play tricks. Then everyone laughs.

4. You can tell a lie on April Fool's Day. If someone believes the lie, say, "April Fool!"

5. Be careful. Someone may tell you a lie. If you believe it, they will say, "April Fool!"

6. Here are some April Fool lies for beginners.

"Your shoe is untied."

"There's a bug on your shoulder."

"There's a spot on your shirt."

"We're having a test today."

"Your car has a flat tire."

"I'm moving away next week."

7. You can play an April Fool's trick: You need a coin or a dollar bill, tape, and thread.

8. Tape a very long thread to the money. Put the money down on the floor or the sidewalk. Hold the other end of the thread. Stand away.

9. When someone sees the money and tries to pick it up, quickly pull the thread. Laugh and say, "April Fool!"

THE STORY OF APRIL FOOL'S DAY

1. No one is sure how April Fool's Day began. There has been silliness in the spring for thousands of years.

2. In April, fish in the rivers are more easily caught. In France, a foolish person who was easily tricked was called an "April fish."

3. In Europe, by the old calendar, the first day of the new year was the same day as the first day of spring. There were many New Year's customs: visiting friends, giving presents, and other happy activities.

4. In 1582 a new, more accurate calendar was made by Pope Gregory. The beginning of the year was changed to January first.

5. But many people continued to celebrate New Year's Day in April. Other people called these people who would not change their calendars "April Fools." They sent funny presents or played tricks on them.

Do you know these words? Find these words in the story. Draw a line under them. Copy the words. Write the meanings.

no one	activities
sure	calendar
silly/silliness	accurate
thousands	continue/continued
fish	celebrate
foolish	play/played tricks
trick/tricked	

APRIL FOOL'S DAY: EXERCISES

I. Do you know these words? Find these words in the story. Draw a line under them. Copy the words. Write the meanings.

fun	trick	shirt
fool	laugh	test
think/thought	beginners	flat tire
carefully	untied	coin
believe	bug	dollar bill
true	shoulder	thread
lie/lies	spot	pick it up

II. Answer:

1. What day is April Fool's Day? _____

2. A fool is a person who easily believes things that are not _____.

3. On April Fool's Day, people tell _____ to fool other people.

4. If someone believes a lie on April Fool's day, you say, "_____ _____!"

5. What are some April Fool lies you can tell to trick people?

_____

_____

_____

_____

_____

III. Discuss:

1. Do you celebrate April Fool's Day in your country?

2. Is there some other day when people play tricks on each other?

3. What kinds of lies are *not* funny on April Fool's Day?

THE PASSOVER SEDER

ALL ABOUT PASSOVER

1. Passover is a holiday for Jewish people. This year Passover is _____ to
_____.

2. Before Passover, Jewish families completely clean their house. They empty and wash every closet. No dirt or dust may remain. No bread or yeast may be in the house.

3. On the first evening of Passover, Jewish families get together. They have a Seder. The Seder is a special way to remember the history of the Jewish people.

4. People wear their best clothes. Men wear small prayer caps called yarmulkes (ýah muh kuhs) on their heads.

5. The table is set very carefully. There are many things on the table.

There is a big bone from a lamb.

There is matzo.

There are boiled eggs.

There are bitter herbs and sweet *charoset.*

There is a cup of salt water.

There is a cup filled with wine for Elijah the Prophet.

6. The youngest child asks questions about this special dinner.

7. Everyone reads from the Haggadah. The Haggadah is the book about the first Passover. Then they enjoy the dinner. They eat matzo instead of bread. They open the door "so Elijah can come in and join the family."

ALL ABOUT PASSOVER: EXERCISES

I. Do you know these words? Find these words in the story. Draw a line under them. Copy the words. Write the meanings.

Passover	empty	egg
holiday	closet	herbs
Jewish	dirt, dust	charoset
family/families	remain	salt
get together	clothes	wine
Seder	prayer caps	prophet
special	bone	young/youngest
remember	lamb	Haggadah
history	matzo	join

II. Match:

1. Seder _____   A. a small cap

2. yarmulke _____   B. a book about the story of Passover

3. matzo _____   C. a Prophet

4. Elijah _____   D. a special dinner for Passover

5. Haggadah _____   E. flat bread

6. Passover is a _____ holiday.   (Christian, Jewish)

7. Before Passover, Jewish families completely clean their _____.

   (house, table)

8. There are many things on the table. There is a bone from a _____.

   (cow, lamb)

9. The _____ child asks questions about this special dinner.

   (oldest, youngest)

10. After they read the story of Passover, they _____. (eat the dinner,

    clean their house completely)

THE STORY OF THE FIRST PASSOVER

1. A very, very long time ago, the Jewish people were slaves in Egypt. They had to work for the king, or Pharaoh. The Egyptians were very cruel to the Jews.

2. Moses was a Jew. One day Moses heard the voice of God. God said, "Go to Pharaoh. Tell Pharaoh to let the Jews leave Egypt."

3. So Moses went to Pharaoh. "Let my people go," he said.

4. "No," said Pharaoh. "Go back to work."

5. Then God turned all the water in Egypt to blood. The rivers turned to blood, and all the fish in the river died. The people could not drink the water.

6. But Pharaoh would not let the Jews leave Egypt.

7. Then God made frogs come up out of the river. Millions of frogs jumped everywhere. Frogs covered the land.

8. Still Pharaoh would not let the Jews leave Egypt.

9. Then God sent gnats. Millions and billions of tiny little gnats flew on all the people and animals.

THE STORY OF THE FIRST PASSOVER (continued)

10. But Pharaoh would not let the Jews leave Egypt.

11. Then God sent flies. Then God killed all the cows and horses and donkeys. Then God made sores on the people's skin, and He sent hail that killed the plants in the field. He sent locusts to eat all the plants. He sent darkness for three days.

12. But Pharaoh would not let the Jews leave Egypt.

13. Finally, God told the Jews to put the blood of a lamb over the doors of the Jewish houses. At night God killed the first-born son of every Egyptian family. But he passed over the doors of the Jewish homes.

14. All the Egyptians were crying. Even the first-born son of Pharaoh was dead. This time Pharaoh said, "The Jews may leave Egypt. Go."

15. The Jews left their homes very quickly. They did not have time to let their bread rise. They followed Moses. They went to the East.

16. Pharaoh saw them go. We need our slaves, he thought. He sent his soldiers to stop the Jews.

17. The Jews were at the Red Sea. God made a wind that divided the waters. The Jews crossed the Red Sea on dry land.

18. Pharaoh's soldiers followed the Jews into the sea. The wind changed. The sea covered Pharaoh and his soldiers. They all died.

19. Every year, Jews remember the Passover. They tell about the flight from Egypt at the Passover Seder.

Name _____ Date _____

THE STORY OF THE FIRST PASSOVER: EXERCISES

I. Do you know these words? Find these words in the story. Draw a line under them. Copy the words. Write the meanings.

slaves	to cover/covered	son
Egypt	land	pass/passed over
Pharaoh	gnats	quickly
cruel	fly/flies	soldiers
voice	sores	sea
God	hail	wind
leave/left	locusts	divide/divided
blood	darkness	cross/crossed
turn water to blood	finally	dry
die/died	lamb	remember
frogs	first-born	flight

II. Choose the best answer:

1. The Jews were slaves in _____. (Egypt, Israel)

2. The king of the Egyptians was _____. (Moses, Pharaoh)

3. God told Moses to tell Pharaoh to let the Jews _____ Egypt. (leave, come to)

4. Pharaoh said, "_____." (Yes, No)

5. God turned the river to _____. (water, blood)

6. God sent _____ and _____ and _____

and _____ and sores on people's skin and three days of _____

and _____ and He killed all the cows and horses and donkeys.

7. But Pharaoh would not let the _____ leave Egypt. (soldiers, Jews)

8. Then the Jews put the _____ of a lamb over their doors. (bones, blood)

9. God killed the first-born sons of the _____. He did not kill the

_____. (Jews, Egyptians)

10. Then _____ said that the Jews could leave. (Pharaoh, God)

THE STORY OF THE FIRST PASSOVER: EXERCISES (continued)

11. The Jews left Egypt very _____. (slowly, quickly)

12. They did not have time to let their _____ rise.   (sun, bread)

13. They came to the Red _____.   (Sea, River)

14. _____ sent a wind that divided the water.   (Pharaoh, God)

15. The Jews crossed over the sea on dry land. Pharaoh's _____ (slaves,

    soldiers) followed them. The wind changed and the sea covered them. Pharaoh's soldiers

    all _____.   (swam, died)

III.   MATCH:

    1. Pharaoh _____   A. leader of the Jews

    2. Moses _____   B. King of the Egyptians

    3. slave _____   C. the oldest boy in a family

    4. hail _____   D. grasshopper

    5. locust _____   E. little balls of ice

    6. first-born son _____   F. a person who is not free and who works without pay

IV.   ACTIVITIES:

Sample some of the foods of the Seder and have a tasting party.

Matzo; bitter herbs: parsley, horseradish

charoset: chopped apple, honey, and nuts

Name _____ Date _____

ALL ABOUT EASTER

1. Easter is a spring holiday. It is a Christian holiday. It is always on a Sunday. This year, Easter is on _____.

2. Christians say Jesus died on Good Friday. On the third day, he rose from the dead. He became alive again.

3. Christians go to church on Easter Sunday. They go at sunrise. They sing and pray.

4. They think about a new life after death. It is a very happy day.

5. Flowers, chicks, eggs, and rabbits are all signs of Easter. They are signs of new life.

6. People are ready for spring. They are happy that winter is over. In some cities, people show their new clothes in an "Easter Parade."

ALL ABOUT EASTER (continued)

7. Little children believe in the Easter Bunny. The Easter Bunny has many baskets.

8. He fills the baskets with colored eggs and candy. Then he hides the baskets.

9. On Easter morning, the children hunt for their baskets.

10. Children color eggs too.

11. They play games with the eggs. They roll eggs up a hill. They have Easter egg or jelly bean hunts.

12. Families eat a big dinner on Easter Sunday.

EASTER: EXERCISES AND ACTIVITIES

I. Do you know these words? Find these words in the story. Draw a line under them. Copy the words. Write the meanings.

Easter	death	Easter Parade
spring	flowers	children
Christian	chicks	Easter Bunny
always	eggs	baskets
Jesus	rabbits	fills
die/died	signs	colored eggs
third	are ready for	hide/hid
rise/rose	winter	hunt for
dead	to be over	games
church	wear	roll
sing	clothes	up hill
pray	show	family/families
life		

II. Choose the best answer:

1. Easter is a _____ holiday.   (Jewish, Christian, Muslim)

2. It is always on a _____.   (Sunday, Tuesday)

3. Christians go to _____ on Easter Sunday.   (church, school)

4. People are ready for _____.   (winter, spring)

5. Flowers, chicks, eggs, and rabbits are all signs of _____.

   (Easter, Christmas)

6. Little children believe in the Easter _____.   (Flower, Bunny)

7. The Easter Bunny fills baskets with colored _____ and

   _____.   (eggs, candy; marbles, flowers)

8. On Easter morning, children hunt for their _____.   (clothes, baskets)

EASTER: EXERCISES AND ACTIVITIES (continued)

III. MATCH:

A. rabbit	B. basket	C. chick
D. egg	E. cross	F. flower

GETTING READY TO COLOR EASTER EGGS

We will color Easter eggs. Bring this page home to get ready.

1. We will color eggs for Easter.

2. Bring two hard-boiled eggs to school on _____.
   (Cook the eggs gently in water for 15 minutes.)

3. Carry the eggs in part of an egg carton. Wrap the eggs carefully so they will not break.

COLORING EASTER EGGS

Do you want to color eggs for Easter? You need:

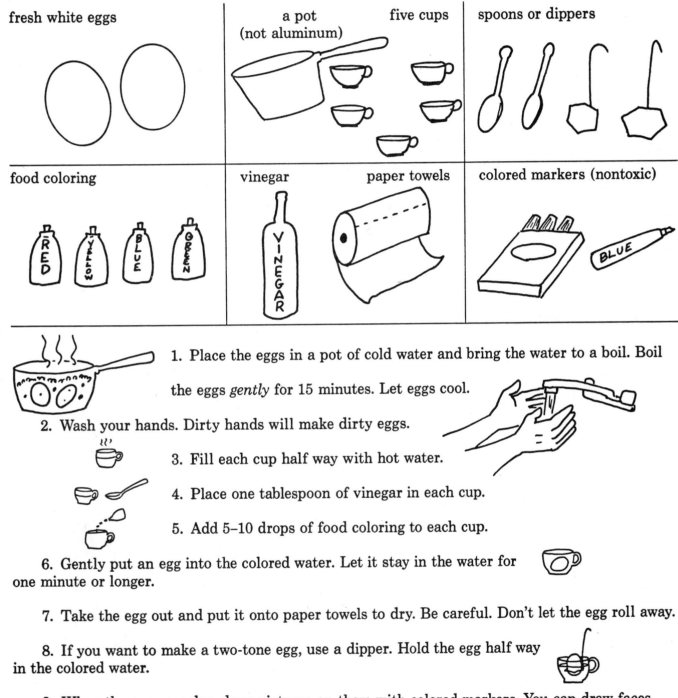

fresh white eggs

a pot (not aluminum)   five cups   spoons or dippers

food coloring   vinegar   paper towels   colored markers (nontoxic)

1. Place the eggs in a pot of cold water and bring the water to a boil. Boil the eggs *gently* for 15 minutes. Let eggs cool.

2. Wash your hands. Dirty hands will make dirty eggs.

3. Fill each cup half way with hot water.

4. Place one tablespoon of vinegar in each cup.

5. Add 5–10 drops of food coloring to each cup.

6. Gently put an egg into the colored water. Let it stay in the water for one minute or longer.

7. Take the egg out and put it onto paper towels to dry. Be careful. Don't let the egg roll away.

8. If you want to make a two-tone egg, use a dipper. Hold the egg half way in the colored water.

9. When the eggs are dry, draw pictures on them with colored markers. You can draw faces, flowers, bunnies, or chicks. You can make designs on the eggs.

10. If you buy Easter egg coloring kits, follow the directions on the kit. Have fun.

COLORING EASTER EGGS: EXERCISES

I. Do you know these words? Find these words in the story. Draw a line under them. Copy the words. Write the meanings.

color	boil	drop
eggs	gently	stay
fresh	minute	dry
pot	cool	be careful
spoon	dirty	two-tone
dipper	fill	design
food coloring	half way	kit
vinegar	hot	
paper towel	tablespoon	

II. What do you do first? Write number 1 on the line next to the sentence. What do you do next? Write number 2, then 3, 4, and 5 next to the sentences where they belong.

_____ Draw pictures on the colored eggs.

_____ Let the eggs cool.

_____ Boil the eggs.

_____ Put the eggs into the colored water.

_____ Put vinegar and drops of food coloring in the cups.

III. Color and decorate these eggs.

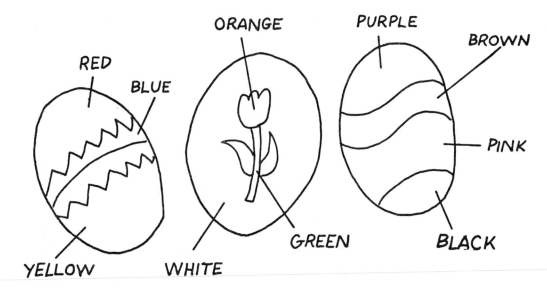

RED   BLUE   ORANGE   PURPLE   BROWN

PINK

YELLOW   WHITE   GREEN   BLACK

DAYLIGHT SAVINGS TIME

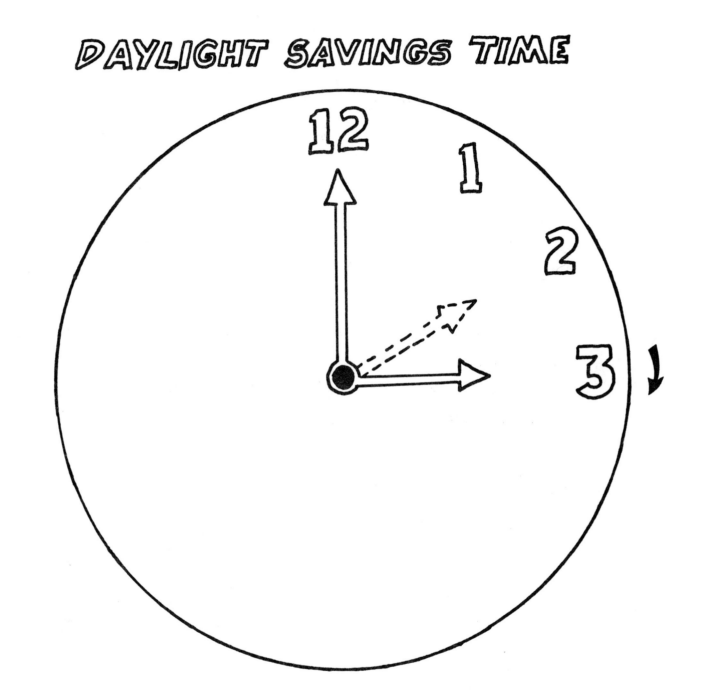

On Sunday, April ———, we turn the clock ahead one hour. This is called Daylight Savings Time. The official clock goes ahead at two A.M. Sunday morning.

MOTHER'S DAY

1. Mother's Day is the second Sunday in May.

2. On Mother's Day, we say thank you to our mothers.

3. On this day, we think about all the work that mothers do.

4. We think about the love that our mothers give us.

5. Children make cards or gifts for their mothers. They can write a thank you letter to their mothers.

6. Children can do their mother's work today. Then mothers can have a day to rest and have fun.

© 1990 by Elizabeth Claire

MOTHER'S DAY: VOCABULARY BUILDING AND ACTIVITIES

I. Do you know these words? Find these words in the story. Draw a line under them. Copy the words. Write the meanings.

mothers	work	letter
second	love	rest
thank you	cards	have fun
think	gifts	

II. Activities:

1. Talk about the things that a mother does for her children. Make a list.

_____

_____

_____

_____

_____

_____

_____

_____

_____

_____

_____

2. Write a letter to your mother, or to the person who does those things for you.

3. In some places people wear carnations to show that they remember their mothers. If their mother is dead, they wear white carnations. If she is alive, they wear pink carnations.

4. Make a gift for your mother.

MEMORIAL DAY

Memorial Day is May ——————————

ALL ABOUT MEMORIAL DAY

1. Memorial Day is a national holiday. It is the fourth Monday of May. This year, Memorial Day is May _____ .

2. On Memorial Day, Americans remember the soldiers who died in wars. There are parades in many towns. Soldiers march in the parades. Bands play marching music.

3. People watch the parades. Then they go to the cemetery. They put flowers and flags on the graves.

4. There is no school on Memorial Day. Banks and post offices are closed.

5. There is a three-day weekend. Many people travel on Memorial Day weekend. Many beaches and parks open for the summer on Memorial Day.

Name —————————————————————— Date ——————————

MEMORIAL DAY: EXERCISES

I. Do you know these words? Find these words in the story. Draw a line under them. Copy the words. Write the meanings.

memorial	wars	graves
national	parades	weekend
holiday	bands	travel
fourth	watch	beach/beaches
remember	cemetery	parks
soldiers	flowers	summer
die/died	flags	

II. Match:

1. soldier _____

2. flag _____

3. grave _____

4. parade _____

5. flowers _____

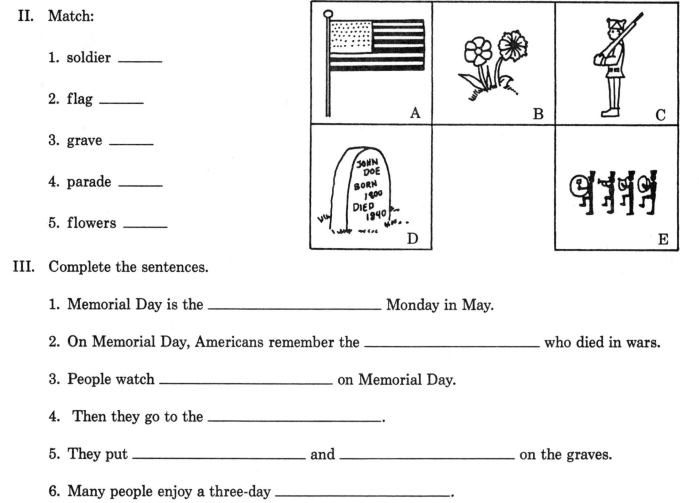

III. Complete the sentences.

1. Memorial Day is the _____ Monday in May.

2. On Memorial Day, Americans remember the _____ who died in wars.

3. People watch _____ on Memorial Day.

4. Then they go to the _____.

5. They put _____ and _____ on the graves.

6. Many people enjoy a three-day _____.

Name _____ Date _____

LET'S TALK ABOUT MEMORIAL DAY

1. What are some of the customs on Memorial Day?

_____

_____

_____

_____

_____

2. What will you and your family do on Memorial Day?

_____

_____

3. Is there a special day in your country to remember dead soldiers?

_____

4. Is there a special day to remember all dead people?

_____

5. Is there a day when people go to temples, churches, or cemeteries to pray for the dead?

_____

6. In the United States, some people are buried. Some are cremated. Some people are put into above-ground mausoleums. Some people donate parts of their bodies to medicine to help others (heart transplants, liver, cornea, and kidney transplants, for example).

What are the customs in your country about dead people?

_____

_____

_____

_____

_____

FLAG DAY

1. Flag Day is June 14. It is a day to honor the American flag.

2. The flag has three colors: red, white and blue. Red is for courage. White is for purity. Blue is for loyalty.

3. There are fifty states in the United States, and fifty stars in the flag.

4. There are thirteen red and white stripes. The stripes are for the thirteen states in 1776, when the United States was a new country.

5. No one is sure who made the first "Stars and Stripes." Most people think it was a woman named Betsy Ross.

6. Show respect for the flag:

    a. Never let the flag touch the floor or the ground.

    b. Fly the flag only in the daytime.

    c. Keep the flag clean.

    d. Do not use the flag to cover a table or for clothing.

    e. Fold the flag carefully when you put it away.

7. Fly the flag on these national holidays:

    a. Memorial Day

    b. Flag Day

    c. Independence Day

    d. Armed Forces Day

    e. Veteran's Day

    f. Washington's Birthday

    g. Lincoln's Birthday

8. When an important American dies, fly the flag "at half mast" (half way up the pole).

9. The flag upside down means distress or danger.

Name _____

Date _____

THE AMERICAN FLAG

185

THE PLEDGE OF ALLEGIANCE

Students in school learn the Pledge of Allegiance. They place their right hand over their heart when they say the Pledge. Soldiers salute the flag.

I pledge allegiance

to the flag

of the United States

of America,

and to the Republic

for which it stands,

one nation,

under God,

indivisible,

with liberty and justice

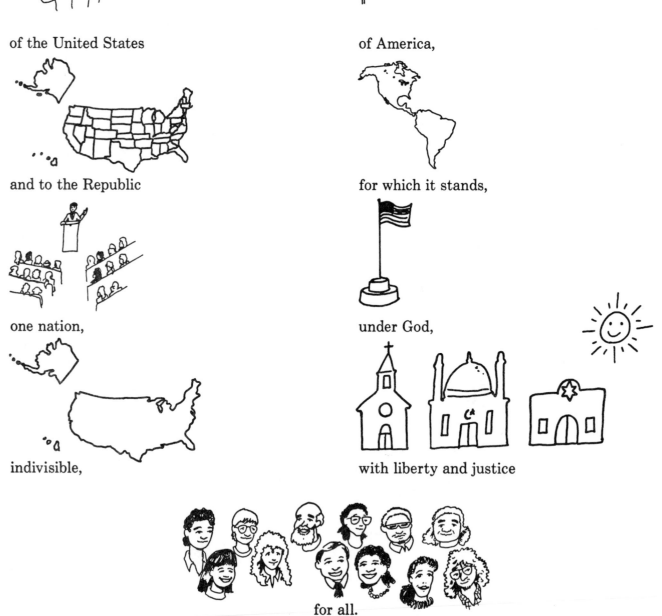

for all.

THE STORY OF THE STAR SPANGLED BANNER

1. In 1814, the United States was at war with England. One terrible battle of the war was fought near Baltimore, Maryland. The English attacked Fort McHenry. The American flag was flying on the fort.

2. Francis Scott Key was an American. He was on a warship. He saw the flag before the sun went down. He watched the battle all night. It was dark, but rockets and bombs were exploding. Sometimes he could see the flag by the light from the bombs and rockets.

3. In the early morning the battle was over. Francis Scott Key looked for the flag. Was it still there? Yes it was. The flag was still waving. It had eleven holes in it, but it was still waving.

4. He was very happy. He wrote a poem. This poem told the feelings of the Americans.

5. The words of the poem fit the music of a song that people knew. People liked Key's song about the "star spangled banner." They started to sing the new words. Congress made this song the National Anthem. This is the official song of the United States.

The Star-Spangled Banner

FRANCIS SCOTT KEY   JOHN STAFFORD SMITH

stream-ing! And the rock-ets' red glare, the bombs burst-ing in

air, Gave_ proof thro' the night_ that our flag was still there.

O_ say, does that_ Star-Span-gled Ban-ner_ yet_

wave_ O'er the land_ of the free and the home of the brave?

189

THE STAR SPANGLED BANNER

Oh say can you see

By the dawn's early light,

What so proudly we hailed

At the twilight's last gleaming?

Whose broad stripes and bright stars

Through the perilous fight

O'er the ramparts we'd watched

Were so gallantly streaming.

And the rocket's red glare,

The bombs bursting in air

Gave proof through the night

That our flag was still there.

O say does that star-spangled banner yet wave

O'er the land of the free

And the home of the brave?

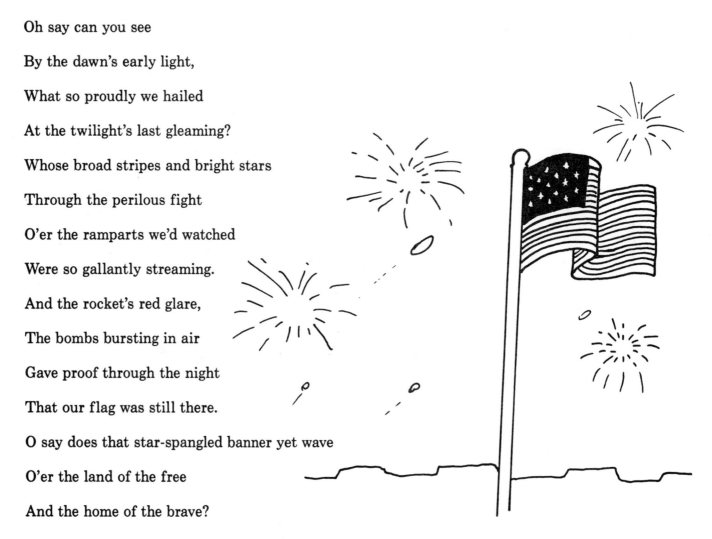

Name _____   Date _____

THE STAR-SPANGLED BANNER: EXERCISES AND ACTIVITIES

I. Do you know these words? Find these words in the story. Draw a line under them. Copy the words. Write the meanings.

star-spangled	wave	gleam/gleaming
banner	hole	broad
war	win/won	stripes
terrible	poem	perilous
battle	feelings	rampart
fight/fought	song	gallant/gallantly
attack/attacked	national anthem	streaming
fort	official	glare
warship	dawn	o'er
rocket	proud/proudly	land
bomb	hail	free
explode	twilight	brave

II. Find a word in "The Star-Spangled Banner" that means the same as:

1. sunrise _____

2. sunset _____

3. wide _____

4. dangerous _____

5. walls of a fort _____

6. bravely _____

7. flying (as a flag) _____

8. bright light _____

9. exploding _____

III. What is "the land of the free, the home of the brave"?

_____

IV. Activities:

1. Practice reciting the Pledge of Allegiance.
2. Learn the proper way to fold a flag.
3. Draw the flag of your country and display it.
4. Sing your national anthem or bring in a recording of it.

FATHER'S DAY

1. Father's Day is the third Sunday in June. It is a special day for fathers.

2. Fathers show their love for their children in many ways. Fathers work to pay for a home and food and clothing.

3. Fathers help take care of the house and the children. Fathers teach their children many things.

4. You can thank your father on Father's Day. Thank him for his love and for the work he does for your family.

FATHER'S DAY: EXERCISES AND ACTIVITIES

I. Do you know these words? Find these words in the story. Draw a line under them. Copy the words. Write the meanings.

third	pay/paid	take care of/took care of
Sunday	home	teach/taught
special	food	thank
show	clothing	work
love	help	family

II. Make a list of the things your father does for you.

_____

_____

_____

_____

_____

_____

_____

_____

_____

_____

III. Activities

1. Write a letter to thank your father.

2. Make a booklet of the things your father does for you.

3. Make a gift for your father.

THE FIRST DAY OF SUMMER

1. Summer begins on June 21. This is the longest day of the year. The night is the shortest.

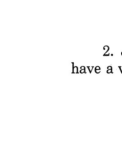

2. July and August are very hot. Most schools have a vacation for the summer.

3. Some children go to summer school. Others go to summer camp or playschool.

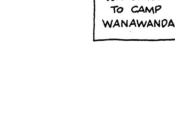

4. Teenagers can get a job for the summer.

5. The beaches are crowded in the summer. So are lakes and parks.

Name _____ Date _____

THE FIRST DAY OF SUMMER: EXERCISES

I. Do you know these words? Find these words in the story. Draw a line under them. Copy the words. Write the meanings.

summer	July	job
June	August	beach
long/longest	hot	crowded
year	vacation	lake
night	summer camp	park
short/shortest	teenagers	

II. Complete:

1. The first day of summer is _____ _____.

2. This is the _____ day of the year.

3. The night is the _____ night of the year.

4. The beaches are _____ in the summer.

5. What will you do this summer?

_____

_____

_____

_____

_____

III. Activities:

1. Make a list of words that remind you of summer such as ice cream, vacation, beach, baseball, fish, and play. Play summertime/vacation bingo.

2. Plan a trip to a zoo, park, or other outdoor area.

3. Have a class picnic.

4. Draw a summer picture.

5. Find out the times for sunrise and sunset in your area. How many hours of daylight are there?

INDEPENDENCE DAY

The United States has a birthday. It is the Fourth of July.

There are parades and picnics on the Fourth of July. At night there are band concerts and fireworks. It is a very happy and noisy holiday.

THE STORY OF INDEPENDENCE DAY

1. More than two hundred years ago, England had thirteen colonies in America. The colonies made England rich. Many Englishmen came to live in the colonies. People came from other countries too.

2. England made laws for the colonies. England collected taxes from the colonies. England sent soldiers to the colonies.

3. The people in the colonies in 1775 did not like the laws. They did not like the taxes. They did not like the English soldiers in their land. They did not like the English king.

4. The American colonists would not pay some taxes. They broke some of the laws.

5. The king wanted to punish the Americans. He sent more soldiers. The soldiers killed some Americans.

6. The Americans began to fight against England.

7. In 1776, the American colonists had a big meeting in Philadelphia. They decided to fight for independence from England. They asked Thomas Jefferson to write a Declaration of Independence.

8. The words Thomas Jefferson wrote are now very famous:

9. ". . . We hold these truths to be self-evident: that all men are created equal, and that they are endowed by their Creator with certain unalienable rights: life, liberty, and the pursuit of happiness. . . .

THE STORY OF INDEPENDENCE DAY (continued)

10. . . . In the name of the good people of these colonies, . . . we declare that these United Colonies are, and of right ought to be free and Independent States . . .

11. And for the support of this declaration, . . . we mutually pledge to each other our lives, our fortunes and our sacred honor."

12. It was very dangerous to sign this declaration. If England won the war, the signers would lose everything, even their lives.

13. John Hancock was the president of the meeting. He was the first one to sign the Declaration of Independence. He wrote his name in big letters to show that he was not afraid.

14. Fifty-five other men signed it too. This was on July Fourth, 1776. Now the fight against England became a war for independence.

15. George Washington was the general of the American army. It was a very difficult war. The Americans lost many battles in the first years.

16. At last they got help from France. The war continued until 1781. The British army surrendered to Washington at Yorktown, Virginia. In 1783, Britain signed the Peace of Paris. The United States was now truly independent.

Name _____   Date _____

INDEPENDENCE DAY: EXERCISES

I. Do you know these words? Find these words in the story. Draw 1 line under them. Copy the words. Write the meanings.

colony/colonies	meeting	free
rich	independence	support
law	declare	mutual/mutually
collect	declaration	pledge
tax/taxes	truth	life/lives
send/sent	self-evident	fortunes
soldiers	create/created	sacred
land	Creator	honor
king	equal	dangerous
pay/paid	endowed	win/won
break/broke	unalienable	sign/signer
punish	rights	lose/lost
kill/killed	liberty	president
begin/began	pursuit	general
fight	happiness	army
against	ought to be	war
colonists	battles	
decide/decided	continued	

II. What's the word?

1. A land that is owned by another country _____

2. Money collected from people by the government _____

3. A person in the army _____

4. Not owned by another country or person _____

5. An announcement; something said firmly and officially _____

6. Easy to see; obvious _____

7. To make _____

8. Cannot be taken away _____

9. Freedom _____

10. Promise _____

11. All the things owned by someone: money, land, property _____

12. To write one's name _____

LET'S TALK ABOUT INDEPENDENCE DAY

I. Answer the questions below:

    1. How many colonies did England have in America? _____

    2. Who made the laws for the colonies? _____

    3. Who collected the taxes? _____

    4. Did the Americans like the laws? _____

    5. Did the Americans like the taxes? _____

    6. Where was the meeting to write the Declaration of Independence? _____

    7. Who wrote the Declaration of Independence? _____

    8. Why was it dangerous to sign the Declaration of Independence? _____

    9. Who was the first person to sign the Declaration of Independence? _____

    10. What day was the Declaration of Independence signed? _____

    11. Who was the general of the American army? _____

    12. What country helped the Americans? _____

    13. When was the war over? _____

II. Discuss the questions below:

    1. Is, or was, your country a colony of another country? _____

    2. Does your country have an Independence Day? _____

    3. When is it? _____

    4. Who are the heroes of independence in your country?

    _____

    5. How do you celebrate your Independence Day?

    _____

    _____

ARBOR DAY

1. Arbor Day is a day to learn about trees and to plant trees. We get many things from trees.

2. Trees are homes for birds, squirrels, and other animals.

3. We can make our homes from trees too.

4. Some trees have fruit that we can eat. We can make maple syrup from the sap of maple trees. We can make paper from trees.

5. Trees can form fences. They protect homes from the wind and from the sun. They hold the soil in the ground when there is a heavy rain. Trees make oxygen for us to breathe.

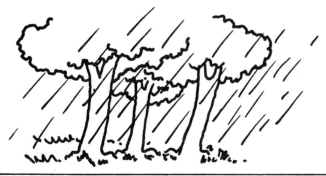

6. Trees are beautiful to look at. Trees give us shade. A tree is great to swing from. Trees are great friends!

7. It takes a long time for a tree to grow. Some of the trees that we enjoy today are fifty or a hundred years old. We must be careful of our trees. We must not cut down too many. We must always plant new trees.

ARBOR DAY: EXERCISES

I. Do you know these words? Find these words in the story. Draw a line under them. Copy the words. Write the meanings.

trees	homes	breathe
protect	wind	shade
plant	hold the soil	swing
squirrels	ground	enjoy
	oxygen	

II. Complete the sentences.

1. Arbor day is _____

_____

2. Trees are homes for _____, squirrels, and other animals.

3. Some trees have _____ that we can eat.

4. We can make maple _____ from the sap of maple trees.

5. Trees protect homes from the _____ and the sun.

6. They hold the _____ in the ground.

7. Trees make _____ for us to breathe.

8. Trees are _____ to look at.

9. It takes a long time for a _____ to grow.

10. We must be _____ of our trees.

11. We must not _____ down too many trees.

12. We must plant new _____.

Name _____   Date _____

TREES

1. There are many, many different kinds of trees.
2. Some trees have broad leaves that fall off before winter comes. These trees are deciduous.
3. Common broad-leaf trees in the United States are maple, oak, chestnut, elm, locust.

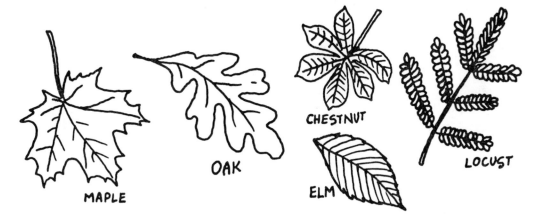

4. Other trees have needles, not leaves. They do not lose the needles in the winter. These trees are called evergreen.
5. Common evergreen trees are pine, spruce, and fir.

6. You can tell the kind of tree by the shape of its leaves. In the winter you can tell the kind of tree by the shape of its branches.

TREES: EXERCISES AND ACTIVITIES

I. Do you know these words? Find these words in the story. Draw a line under them. Copy the words. Write the meanings.

broad	lose	locust
leaf/leaves	evergreen	pine
fall off	common	spruce
winter	maple	fir
deciduous	oak	shape
needles	chestnut	branch/branches
	elm	

II. Answer:

1. Trees that have broad leaves which fall off in the fall are called _____.

2. The maple and oak are _____ leaf trees.

3. Evergreen trees do not have broad leaves. They have _____.

4. Pine trees, spruce trees, and fir trees are _____.

5. In the winter, you can tell what kind of tree it is by the shape of its _____.

III. Activities

1. Collect leaves and place them under a sheet of plain paper. Rub the edge of a crayon over the leaves to make an impression of the veins in the leaf. Compare different leaves.

2. Plant seeds from fruits, or acorns, or other seeds of trees.

3. Take a walk to identify the trees near the school.

4. Tell all the things that trees can do for us.

5. Read the poem "Trees" by Joyce Kilmer.

A HOLIDAY IN MY COUNTRY

1. Name of Holiday: _____

2. Date: _____

3. Is this holiday the birthday of some special person? _____

   (Who? _____)

4. Is it the anniversary of something special that happened? _____

   (What? _____)

5. Is it connected with the change of the seasons, with planting or the harvest? _____

6. Does everyone in the country celebrate this holiday, or is it for one group of people? _____

7. What special clothes do people wear on this day? _____

   _____

8. What special food do people eat? _____

   _____

9. Do people go to a temple or church? _____

10. Do people sing special songs or say special poems or prayers? _____

11. Do people have a big dinner or party? _____

12. Do people decorate their homes or the town? _____

13. Are there special activities at school? _____

14. Do people send cards or exchange gifts? _____

15. What other things do people do?

   _____

   _____

   _____

   _____

A HOLIDAY IN _____
(your country)

A special day in my country is _____. It is

on _____.

On this day, _____

_____

_____

_____

_____

_____

_____

_____

_____

_____

_____

_____

_____

_____

_____

_____

Holiday Activities:

1. Draw a picture of this holiday.
2. Bring in food for the class to taste.
3. Make a "Find-A-Word" puzzle with your holiday words. Make copies for your classmates.

BIRTHDAYS IN THE UNITED STATES

ALL ABOUT BIRTHDAYS

1. My birthday is

   _____.

2. In the United States, birthdays are happy days. Children get presents from their parents.

3. Everyone says "happy birthday" to the birthday person. People send cards to their friends on their birthdays.

4. Sometimes there is a party with a birthday cake. There are candles on the cake. There is one candle for each year, plus one candle "to grow on."

5. The candles are lit. The lights are turned off. Everyone starts to sing,

   Happy birthday to you.
   Happy birthday to you.
   Happy birthday dear _____.
   Happy birthday to you.

   How old are you now?
   How old are you now?
   How old are you _____?
   How old are you now?

6. The birthday person makes a wish. Then she or he blows out the candles.

7. Someone very lightly spanks the birthday person for good luck. If she/he is nine years old, he gets ten spanks. (One is to grow on.)

8. A favorite game at children's birthdays is "Pin the Tail on the Donkey." A blindfold is put on. Then the person has to pin the tail on a picture of a donkey. The one who gets the tail closest to the right place wins a prize.

9. Some people believe that your future can be told by your birth "sign."

ALL ABOUT BIRTHDAYS: EXERCISES AND ACTIVITIES

I. Do you know these words? Find these words in the story. Draw a line under them. Copy the words. Write the meanings.

birthday	blindfold
party	tail
present	donkey
cake	pin
candle	prize
surprise	birth sign

II. Choose the best answer:

1. In the United States, birthdays are _____ days.   (sad, happy)

2. Children get _____ on their birthday.   (presents, candles)

3. On the birthday cake, there is one candle for each _____ (present, child, year) plus one to grow on.

4. If a child is ten years old, he or she gets _____ spanks. (eleven, ten, nine)

5. A favorite game is "Pin the _____ on the Donkey."   (Tail, Leg, Blindfold)

6. The person who gets the tail closest to the _____ (cake, present, right place) wins a prize.

7. What is your birth sign?

March 21 to April 20:	Aries the Ram
April 21 to May 20:	Taurus the Bull
May 21 to June 20:	Gemini the Twins
June 21 to July 20:	Cancer the Crab
July 21 to August 21:	Leo the Lion
August 21 to September 20:	Virgo the Virgin
September 21 to October 20:	Libra the Scales
October 21 to November 20:	Scorpio the Scorpion
November 21 to December 20:	Sagittarius the Archer
December 21 to January 20:	Capricorn the Goat
January 21 to February 20:	Aquarius the Water Bearer
February 21 to March 20:	Pisces the Fish

PRESIDENTS FIND-A-WORD (page 145)

```
W  H  L  G  E  O  S  O  H  O  N  I  N  G
A  A  P  E  W  B  Y  S  O  U  T  H  S  L
S  N  R  O  A  I  S  L  N  L  A  V  L  I
L  E  P  R  E  S  I  D  E  N  T  P  A  R
M  L  T  G  T  R  A  V  S  R  E  S  V  T
T  R  S  E  H  N  O  R  T  H  I  D  E  B
R  O  R  W  D  A  E  S  N  O  R  S  S  I
A  B  R  A  H  A  M  L  I  N  C  O  L  N
M  I  N  S  A  B  R  E  N  T  O  C  E  R
E  R  O  H  A  H  A  M  E  F  U  I  A  L
L  T  R  I  L  I  N  E  R  E  N  V  D  I
I  H  S  N  C  O  R  L  N  E  T  B  E  V
T  D  O  G  C  F  A  T  H  E  R  I  R  I
Q  A  U  T  G  E  O  R  A  B  Y  R  A  C
R  Y  T  O  H  A  M  L  I  H  O  N  S  O
S  T  I  N  D  E  P  E  N  D  E  N  C  E
```

210

WHAT DANGEROUS CONDITIONS
DO YOU SEE IN THIS HOME? (page 30)

a. A baby is playing with matches.
b. Curtains can blow over the stove and catch fire.
c. The toaster has papers on it.
d. There are too many plugs in one outlet.
e. The wire on the lamp is exposed.
f. The pot handle is turned out.
g. The fire extinguisher is near the stove. (If there is a fire, you can't reach the fire extinguisher.)

WHAT'S WRONG WITH THIS PICTURE? (page 158)

a. The car has a foot (instead of a tire).
b. A dog is in the tree.
c. The dog is afraid of the cat.
d. The cat is saying "woof woof" (instead of "meow").
e. A flower is growing in the street.
f. There are two different kinds of flowers on one plant.
g. The flag is backwards.
h. The girl has one long sleeve and one short sleeve.
i. The girl has one long sock and one short sock.
j. The girl has two different shoes.
k. The door is high up and the windows are low.
l. The chimney is on the ground (instead of on the roof).
m. There is a fish in the car.